Addition and Subtraction

Putting Together and Taking Apart

Grade 2

Also appropriate for Grade 3

Karen Economopoulos
Susan Jo Russell

Developed at TERC, Cambridge, Massachusetts

Dale Seymour Publications®
Menlo Park, California

The *Investigations* curriculum was developed at TERC (formerly
Technical Education Research Centers) in collaboration with Kent State
University and the State University of New York at Buffalo. The work was
supported in part by National Science Foundation Grant No. ESI-9050210.
TERC is a nonprofit company working to improve mathematics and science
education. TERC is located at 2067 Massachusetts Avenue, Cambridge,
MA 02140.

**This project was supported, in part,
by the**

National Science Foundation

Opinions expressed are those of the authors
and not necessarily those of the Foundation

Managing Editor: Catherine Anderson
Grade-Level Editor: Alison Abrohms
Series Editor: Beverly Cory
Revision Team: Laura Marshall Alavosus, Ellen Harding, Patty Green Holubar,
Suzanne Knott, Beverly Hersh Lozoff
ESL Consultant: Nancy Sokol Green
Production/Manufacturing Director: Janet Yearian
Production/Manufacturing Coordinator: Amy Changar, Shannon Miller
Design Manager: Jeff Kelly
Design: Don Taka
Illustrations: Laurie Harden, Susan Jaekel, Meryl Treatner
Cover: Bay Graphics
Composition: Archetype Book Composition

This book is published by Dale Seymour Publications®, an imprint of
Addison Wesley Longman, Inc.

Dale Seymour Publications
2725 Sand Hill Road
Menlo Park, CA 94025
Customer Service: 800-872-1100

**DALE
SEYMOUR
PUBLICATIONS®**

Order number DS43804
ISBN 1-57232-657-3
1 2 3 4 5 6 7 8 9 10-ML-01 00 99 98 97

Printed on Recycled Paper

T E R C

Principal Investigator   Susan Jo Russell

Co-Principal Investigator   Cornelia C. Tierney

Director of Research and Evaluation   Jan Mokros

Director of K–2 Curriculum   Karen Economopoulos

Curriculum Development

Joan Akers
Michael T. Battista
Mary Berle-Carman
Douglas H. Clements
Karen Economopoulos
Anne Goodrow
Marlene Kliman
Jerrie Moffett
Megan Murray
Ricardo Nemirovsky
Andee Rubin
Susan Jo Russell
Cornelia C. Tierney
Tracey Wright

Evaluation and Assessment

Mary Berle-Carman
Jan Mokros
Andee Rubin

Teacher Support

Anne Goodrow
Liana Laughlin
Jerrie Moffett
Megan Murray
Tracey Wright

Technology Development

Michael T. Battista
Douglas H. Clements
Julie Sarama

Video Production

David A. Smith
Judy Storeygard

Administration and Production

Irene Baker
Amy Catlin
Amy Taber

**Cooperating Classrooms
for This Unit**

Rose Christiansen
Brookline Public Schools
Brookline, MA

Lisa Seyferth
Carol Walker
Newton Public Schools
Newton, MA

Phyllis Ollove
Boston Public Schools
Boston, MA

Margaret M. McGaffigan
Nashoba Regional School District
Stow, MA

Consultants and Advisors

Deborah Lowenberg Ball
Marilyn Burns
Ann Grady
James J. Kaput
Mary M. Lindquist
John Olive
Leslie P. Steffe
Grayson Wheatley

Graduate Assistants

Kent State University

Kathryn Battista
Caroline Borrow
Judy Norris

State University of New York at Buffalo

Julie Sarama
Sudha Swaminathan
Elaine Vukelic

Revisions and Home Materials

Cathy Miles Grant
Marlene Kliman
Margaret McGaffigan
Megan Murray
Kim O'Neil
Andee Rubin
Susan Jo Russell
Lisa Seyferth
Myriam Steinback
Judy Storeygard
Anna Suarez
Cornelia Tierney
Carol Walker
Tracey Wright

CONTENTS

TEACHER NOTES

WHERE TO START

The first-time user of *Putting Together and Taking Apart* should read the following:

When you next teach this same unit, you can begin to read more of the background. Each time you present the unit, you will learn more about how your students understand the mathematical ideas.

Investigations in Number, Data, and Space® is a K–5 mathematics curriculum with four major goals:

- to offer students meaningful mathematical problems
- to emphasize depth in mathematical thinking rather than superficial exposure to a series of fragmented topics
- to communicate mathematics content and pedagogy to teachers
- to substantially expand the pool of mathematically literate students

The *Investigations* curriculum embodies a new approach based on years of research about how children learn mathematics. Each grade level consists of a set of separate units, each offering 2–8 weeks of work. These units of study are presented through investigations that involve students in the exploration of major mathematical ideas.

Approaching the mathematics content through investigations helps students develop flexibility and confidence in approaching problems, fluency in using mathematical skills and tools to solve problems, and proficiency in evaluating their solutions. Students also build a repertoire of ways to communicate about their mathematical thinking, while their enjoyment and appreciation of mathematics grows.

The investigations are carefully designed to invite all students into mathematics—girls and boys, members of diverse cultural, ethnic, and language groups, and students with different strengths and interests. Problem contexts often call on students to share experiences from their family, culture, or community. The curriculum eliminates barriers— such as work in isolation from peers, or emphasis on speed and memorization—that exclude some students from participating successfully in mathematics. The following aspects of the curriculum ensure that all students are included in significant mathematics learning:

- Students spend time exploring problems in depth.
- They find more than one solution to many of the problems they work on.

- They invent their own strategies and approaches, rather than relying on memorized procedures.
- They choose from a variety of concrete materials and appropriate technology, including calculators, as a natural part of their everyday mathematical work.
- They express their mathematical thinking through drawing, writing, and talking.
- They work in a variety of groupings—as a whole class, individually, in pairs, and in small groups.
- They move around the classroom as they explore the mathematics in their environment and talk with their peers.

While reading and other language activities are typically given a great deal of time and emphasis in elementary classrooms, mathematics often does not get the time it needs. If students are to experience mathematics in depth, they must have enough time to become engaged in real mathematical problems. We believe that a minimum of five hours of mathematics classroom time a week—about an hour a day—is critical at the elementary level. The plan and pacing of the *Investigations* curriculum is based on that belief.

We explain more about the pedagogy and principles that underlie these investigations in Teacher Notes throughout the units. For correlations of the curriculum to the NCTM Standards and further help in using this research-based program for teaching mathematics, see the following books:

- *Implementing the* Investigations in Number, Data, and Space® *Curriculum*
- *Beyond Arithmetic: Changing Mathematics in the Elementary Classroom* by Jan Mokros, Susan Jo Russell, and Karen Economopoulos

This book is one of the curriculum units for *Investigations in Number, Data, and Space.* In addition to providing part of a complete mathematics curriculum for your students, this unit offers information to support your own professional development. You, the teacher, are the person who will make this curriculum come alive in the classroom; the book for each unit is your main support system.

Although the curriculum does not include student textbooks, reproducible sheets for student work are provided in the unit and are also available as Student Activity Booklets. Students work actively with objects and experiences in their own environment and with a variety of manipulative materials and technology, rather than with a book of instruction and problems. We strongly recommend use of the overhead projector as a way to present problems, to focus group discussion, and to help students share ideas and strategies.

Ultimately, every teacher will use these investigations in ways that make sense for his or her particular style, the particular group of students, and the constraints and supports of a particular school environment. Each unit offers information and guidance for a wide variety of situations, drawn from our collaborations with many teachers and students over many years. Our goal in this book is to help you, a professional educator, implement this curriculum in a way that will give all your students access to mathematical power.

Investigation Format

The opening two pages of each investigation help you get ready for the work that follows.

What Happens This gives a synopsis of each session or block of sessions.

Mathematical Emphasis This lists the most important ideas and processes students will encounter in this investigation.

What to Plan Ahead of Time These lists alert you to materials to gather, sheets to duplicate, transparencies to make, and anything else you need to do before starting.

INVESTIGATION 1

Combining and Separating

What Happens

Session 1: Introducing Combining Situations
Students solve a combining problem and record their solutions so that someone else can understand them. Strategies are shared and recorded.

Session 2: Introducing Separating Situations
Students solve a separating problem, using their own strategies. Again, they record their solutions so that someone else can understand them. As a group, students share some of their strategies while you record.

Sessions 3 and 4: Making Sense of Addition and Subtraction Students solve a variety of story problems involving combining and separating, using their own strategies. Their job is to solve problems, check their solutions, and clearly record their approaches. Students are introduced to a new problem structure: combining with an unknown change.

Sessions 5 and 6: Writing Stories for Numerical Problems Students write stories to fit numerical situations such as 28 + 15 or 33 – 18. They are introduced to both horizontal and vertical notation for recording addition and subtraction. They also continue to work on story problems. This is used as a Teacher Checkpoint opportunity.

Mathematical Emphasis

■ Developing models of addition and subtraction situations

■ Solving problems using numerical reasoning

■ Recording solution strategies clearly

■ Considering the relationship between addition and subtraction

■ Understanding horizontal and vertical notation for addition and subtraction

■ Matching addition and subtraction notation to situations they could represent

What to Plan Ahead of Time

Materials

■ Counters such as interlocking cubes, color tiles, or other materials (All Sessions)

■ Student math folders: 1 per student (Session 1)

■ Envelopes: about 12 (Sessions 3–6)

■ Paste or glue sticks (Sessions 3–6)

Other Preparation

■ Duplicate student sheets and teaching resources, located at the end of this unit, in the following quantities. If you have Student Activity Booklets, copy only the item marked with an asterisk.

For Session 1
Student Sheet 1, Weekly Log (p. 148): 1 per student. At this time, you may wish to duplicate a supply to last for the entire unit and distribute the sheets as needed.

Continued on next page

INVESTIGATION 1

What to Plan Ahead of Time (continued)

Family letter* (p. 147): 1 per student. Be sure to sign and date the letter before copying.

Student Sheet 2, Story Problems, Set A (p. 149) or copies of problems you have created: 1 per student

Student Sheet 3, An Addition Story Problem (p. 150): 1 per student (homework)

For Session 2
Student Sheet 4, Story Problems, Set B (p. 151) or copies of problems you have created: 1 per student

Student Sheet 5, A Subtraction Story Problem (p. 152): 1 per student (homework)

For Sessions 3–4
Story Problems, Set C (p. 157) or copies of problems you have created: 1 per student and 1 extra. Cut the sheets apart into individual problems. Store the copies of each problem in a separate envelope. Paste an example of each problem on the front of the envelope so students can see which problem they are choosing.

Student Sheet 6, Story Problems, Set D (p. 153) or copies of problems you have created: 1 per student

Student Sheet 7, Discussing Addition and Subtraction (p. 154): 1 per student (homework)

For Sessions 5–6
Story Problems, Set E (p. 159) or copies of problems you have created: 1 per student

Cut apart into individual problems. Store copies of each problem in a separate envelope.

Student Sheet 8, Problem Strategies (p. 155): 2 per student (homework)

Student Sheet 9, Writing and Solving a Story Problem (p. 156): 1 per student (homework)

■ Think about situations familiar to students that you might use as contexts for addition and subtraction problems. Throughout this unit, you may want to substitute problems of your own. For more information, see the **Teacher Note**, Creating Your Own Story Problems (p. 11). If you use your own problem contexts, create the following kinds of problems: a combining problem (with follow-up) for Session 1, a separating problem (with follow-up) for Session 2, a mixture of 6–8 problems for Sessions 3 and 4 (combining and separating with unknown outcomes) a combining problem with unknown change (with follow-up) for Session 4, and two combining problems with unknown change (with follow-ups) for Sessions 5 and 6. See the **Teacher Note**, Types of Story Problems: Combining and Separating (p. 13) for more information about problem types.

■ Prepare a math folder for each student, if this was not done for a previous unit. (Session 1)

Sessions Within an investigation, the activities are organized by class session, a session being at least a one-hour math class. Sessions are numbered consecutively through an investigation. Often several sessions are grouped together, presenting a block of activities with a single major focus.

When you find a block of sessions presented together—for example, Sessions 1, 2, and 3—read through the entire block first to understand the overall flow and sequence of the activities. Make some preliminary decisions about how you will divide the activities into three sessions for your class, based on what you know about your students. You may need to modify your initial plans as you progress through the activities, and you may want to make notes in the margins of the pages as reminders for the next time you use the unit.

Be sure to read the Session Follow-Up section at the end of the session block to see what homework assignments and extensions are suggested as you make your initial plans.

While you may be used to a curriculum that tells you exactly what each class session should cover, we have found that the teacher is in a better position to make these decisions. Each unit is flexible and may be handled somewhat differently by every teacher. While we provide guidance for how many sessions a particular group of activities is likely to need, we want you to be active in determining an appropriate pace and the best transition points for your class. It is not unusual for a teacher to spend more or less time than is proposed for the activities.

Classroom Routines The Start-Up at the beginning of each session offers suggestions for how to acknowledge and integrate homework from the previous session, and which Classroom Routine activities to include sometime during the school day. Routines provide students with regular practice in important mathematical skills such as solving number combinations, collecting and organizing data, understanding time, and seeing spatial relationships. Two routines, How Many Pockets? and Today's Number, are used regularly in the grade 2 *Investigations* units. A third routine, Time and Time Again, appears in the final unit, *Timelines and Rhythm Patterns*. This routine provides a variety of activities about understanding

---

Session 2

Introducing Separating Situations

Materials

■ Counters
■ Student Sheet 4 (1 per student)
■ Student Sheet 5 (1 per student, homework)

What Happens

Students solve a separating problem, using their own strategies. Again, they record their solutions so that someone else can understand them. As a group, students share some of their strategies while you record. Their work focuses on:

■ visualizing separating situations
■ developing strategies for separating
■ recording strategies clearly

Start-Up

Combining Problem Ask students about their experience writing problems for homework. You may choose to collect students' work and look at their problems to give you a sense of whether students were able to create a combining situation that matched an addition expression.

Today's Number

■ **Calendar Date** If you are using the calendar date for Today's Number, brainstorm with students ways to express the number. Record students' expressions on chart paper so that they can be saved each day.

■ **Number of School Days** If you are using the number of school days as Today's Number, and the number is over 100, encourage students to break the number into parts such as 100 + 10, then offer suggestions for how to express one of those numbers, keeping the other intact. For example: 100 + 5 + 5 or 100 + 4 + 4 + 2. Add a card to the class counting strip and fill in another number on the blank 200 chart.

Activity

Problems About Separating

This session focuses on separating situations and is parallel to Session 1, Introducing Combining Situations. Introduce a problem such as the one below to the whole class. As in Session 1, you may want to change the context of the problem so that it is more familiar to students. Keep the same numbers and the basic structure of the problem. The Teacher Notes, Creating Your Own Story Problems (p. 11) and Types of Story Problems: Combining and Separating (p. 13), provide help for developing your own problems.

20 ■ *Investigation 1: Combining and Separating*

---

time; these can be easily integrated throughout the school day and into other parts of the classroom curriculum. A fourth routine, Quick Images, supports work in the unit *Shapes, Halves, and Symmetry*. After its introduction, you might do it once or twice a week to develop students' visual sense of number (as displayed in dot arrangements).

Most Classroom Routine activities are short and can be done whenever you have a spare 10 minutes—maybe before lunch or recess, or at the beginning or end of the day. Complete descriptions of the Classroom Routines can be found at the end of the units.

Activities The activities include pair and small-group work, individual tasks, and whole-class discussions. In any case, students are seated together, talking and sharing ideas during all work times. Students most often work cooperatively, although each student may record work individually.

Choice Time In most units, some sessions are structured with activity choices. In these cases, students may work simultaneously on different activities focused on the same mathematical ideas. Students choose which activities they want to do, and they cycle through them.

You will need to decide how to set up and introduce these activities and how to let students make their choices. Some teachers set up choices as stations around the room, while others post the list of available choices and allow students to collect their own materials and choose their own work space. You may need to experiment with a few different structures before finding a set up that works best for you, your students, and your classroom.

Extensions Sometimes in Session Follow-Up, you will find suggested extension activities. These are opportunities for some or all students to explore a topic in greater depth or in a different context. They are not designed for "fast" students; mathematics is a multifaceted discipline, and different students will want to go further in different investigations. Look for and encourage the sparks of interest and enthusiasm you see in your students, and use the extensions to help them pursue these interests.

Excursions Some of the *Investigations* units include excursions—blocks of activities that could be omitted without harming the integrity of the unit. This is one way of dealing with the great depth and variety of elementary mathematics—much more than a class has time to explore in any one year. Excursions give you the flexibility to make different choices from year to year, doing the excursion in one unit this time, and next year trying another excursion.

Tips for the Linguistically Diverse Classroom At strategic points in each unit, you will find concrete suggestions for simple modifications of the teaching strategies to encourage the participation of all students. Many of these tips offer alternative ways to elicit critical thinking from students at varying levels of English proficiency, as well as from other students who find it difficult to verbalize their thinking.

The tips are supported by suggestions for specific vocabulary work to help ensure that all students can participate fully in the investigations. The Preview for the Linguistically Diverse Classroom (p. I-24) lists important words that are assumed

as part of the working vocabulary of the unit. Second-language learners will need to become familiar with these words in order to understand the problems and activities they will be doing. These terms can be incorporated into students' second-language work before or during the unit. Activities that can be used to present the words are found in the appendix, Vocabulary Support for Second-Language Learners (p. 144). In addition, ideas for making connections to students' language and cultures, included on the Preview page, help the class explore the unit's concepts from a multicultural perspective.

Materials

A complete list of the materials needed for teaching this unit is found on p. I-18. Some of these materials are available in kits for the *Investigations* curriculum. Individual items can also be purchased from school supply dealers.

Classroom Materials In an active mathematics classroom, certain basic materials should be available at all times: interlocking cubes, pencils, unlined paper, graph paper, calculators, and things to count with. Some activities in this curriculum require scissors and glue sticks or tape. Stick-on notes and large paper are also useful materials throughout.

So that students can independently get what they need at any time, they should know where these materials are kept, how they are stored, and how they are to be returned to the storage area. Many teachers have found that stopping 5 minutes before the end of each session so that students can finish their work and clean up is helpful in maintaining classroom materials. You'll find that establishing such routines at the beginning of the year is well worth the time and effort.

Technology Calculators are introduced to students in the second unit of the grade 2 sequence, *Coins, Coupons, and Combinations.* It is assumed that calculators are readily available throughout the curriculum.

Computer activities at grade 2 use two software programs that were developed especially for the *Investigations* curriculum. The program *Shapes* is used in the introductory unit, *Mathematical Thinking at Grade 2,* and again during the geometry and fractions unit, *Shapes, Halves, and Symmetry.* Geo-Logo™ is introduced and used in the measurement unit, *How Long? How Far?* Although the software is linked to activities only in these three units, we recommend that students use it throughout the year. As students use the software over time, they continue to develop skills presented in the units. How you incorporate the computer activities into your curriculum depends on the number of computers you have available. Suggestions are offered in the geometry unit for how to organize different types of computer environments.

Children's Literature Each unit offers a list of suggested children's literature (p. I-18) that can be used to support the mathematical ideas in the unit. Sometimes an activity is based on a selected children's book, with suggestions for substitutions where practical. While such activities can be adapted and taught without the book, the literature offers a rich introduction and should be used whenever possible.

Student Sheets and Teaching Resources Student recording sheets and other teaching tools needed for both class and homework are provided as reproducible blackline masters at the end of each unit. They are also available as Student Activity Booklets. These booklets contain all the sheets

each student will need for individual work, freeing you from extensive copying (although you may need or want to copy the occasional teaching resource on transparency film or card stock, or make extra copies of a student sheet).

We think it's important that students find their own ways of organizing and recording their work. They need to learn how to explain their thinking with both drawings and written words, and how to organize their results so someone else can understand them. For this reason, we deliberately do not provide student sheets for every activity. Regardless of the form in which students do their work, we recommend that they keep a mathematics notebook or folder so that their work is always available for reference.

Homework In *Investigations,* homework is an extension of classroom work. Sometimes it offers review and practice of work done in class, sometimes preparation for upcoming activities, and sometimes numerical practice that revisits work in earlier units. Homework plays a role both in supporting students' learning and in helping inform families about the ways in which students in this curriculum work with mathematical ideas.

Depending on your school's homework policies and your own judgment, you may want to assign more homework than is suggested in the units. For this purpose you might use the practice pages, included as blackline masters at the end of this unit, to give students additional work with numbers.

For some homework assignments, you will want to adapt the activity to meet the needs of a variety of students in your class: those with special needs, those ready for more challenge, and second-language learners. You might change the numbers in a problem, make the activity more or less complex, or go through a sample activity with those who need extra help. You can modify any student sheet for either homework or class use. In particular, making numbers in a problem smaller or larger can make the same basic activity appropriate for a wider range of students.

Another issue to consider is how to handle the homework that students bring back to class—how to recognize the work they have done at home without spending too much time on it. Some teachers hold a short group discussion of different approaches to the assignment; others ask students to share and discuss their work with a neighbor, or post the homework around the room and give students time to tour it briefly. If you want to keep track of homework students bring in, be sure it ends up in a designated place.

Investigations at Home It is a good idea to make your policy on homework explicit to both students and their families when you begin teaching with *Investigations*. How frequently will you be assigning homework? When do you expect homework to be completed and brought back to school? What are your goals in assigning homework? How independent should families expect their children to be? What should the parent's or guardian's role be? The more explicit you can be about your expectations, the better the homework experience will be for everyone.

Investigations at Home (a booklet available separately for each unit, to send home with students) gives you a way to communicate with families about the work students are doing in class. This

booklet includes a brief description of every session, a list of the mathematics content emphasized in each investigation, and a discussion of each homework assignment to help families more effectively support their children. Whether or not you are using the *Investigations* at Home booklets, we expect you to make your own choices about homework assignments. Feel free to omit any and to add extra ones you think are appropriate.

Family Letter A letter that you can send home to students' families is included with the blackline masters for each unit. Families need to be informed about the mathematics work in your classroom; they should be encouraged to participate in and support their children's work. A reminder to send home the letter for each unit appears in one of the early investigations. These letters are also available separately in Spanish, Vietnamese, Cantonese, Hmong, and Cambodian.

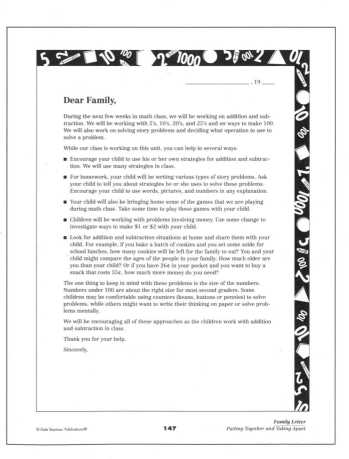

Help for You, the Teacher

Because we believe strongly that a new curriculum must help teachers think in new ways about mathematics and about their students' mathematical thinking processes, we have included a great deal of material to help you learn more about both.

About the Mathematics in This Unit This introductory section (p. I-19) summarizes the critical information about the mathematics you will be teaching. It describes the unit's central mathematical ideas and how students will encounter them through the unit's activities.

Teacher Notes These reference notes provide practical information about the mathematics you are teaching and about our experience with how students learn. Many of the notes were written in response to actual questions from teachers, or to discuss important things we saw happening in the field-test classrooms. Some teachers like to read them all before starting the unit, then review them as they come up in particular investigations.

Dialogue Boxes Sample dialogues demonstrate how students typically express their mathematical ideas, what issues and confusions arise in their thinking, and how some teachers have guided class discussions.

These dialogues are based on the extensive classroom testing of this curriculum; many are word-for-word transcriptions of recorded class discussions. They are not always easy reading; sometimes it may take some effort to unravel what the students are trying to say. But this is the value of these dialogues; they offer good clues to how your students may develop and express their approaches and strategies, helping you prepare for your own class discussions.

Where to Start You may not have time to read everything the first time you use this unit. As a first-time user, you will likely focus on understanding the activities and working them out with your students. Read completely through each investigation before starting to present it. Also read those sections listed in the Contents under the heading Where to Start (p. vi).

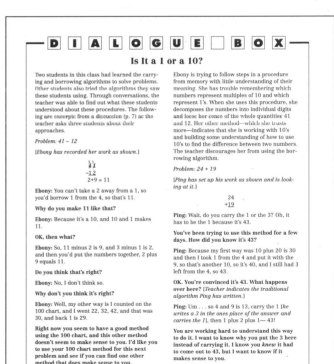

Types of Story Problems: Combining and Separating ◁ Teacher Note

In the elementary grades, students are often exposed to only a few types of story problems. The two problem types that are most familiar are addition of two quantities to find a total and subtraction in which one quantity is removed from another.

Current research has focused on how students in the primary grades solve addition and subtraction problems. One outcome of this research has been to identify the variety of problem types that students should encounter in the elementary grades. Students usually do not encounter a wide enough variety of problem structures and therefore have a limited idea of how to apply addition and subtraction to solve word problems.

In this unit, students will encounter three basic problem structures—combining, separating, and comparing. This note describes combining and separating, which are introduced in Investigations 1 and 3. Comparing situations will be introduced in Investigation 5 and are discussed in the **Teacher Note**, Types of Story Problems: Comparing (p. 109).

Combining These are problems in which two quantities are combined to form a third quantity. Called *joining* or *combining* problems, these include familiar addition situations such as:

Ted had 6 marbles.
Sophia gave him 4 more.
How many does Ted have now?

In this combining situation, the two quantities to be combined are known, and their sum is to be found. These are problems with an *unknown outcome*—the parts are combined and the outcome of that combining action, the total, is unknown. However, it is also important that students encounter combining situations in which the whole and one quantity are known and the second quantity must be found:

Ted had 6 marbles. Sophia gave him some.
Now Ted has 10 marbles.
How many did Sophia give him?

How the problem is solved is not what determines whether this is a combining problem. Some students might solve it by subtracting 6 from 10; others might think of it as, "What do I need to add to 6 to get 10?" However it is solved, the structure is considered combining—two quantities are combined to create a third. In this case the *outcome* is known, but the *change* that occurs—what was added to 6—is not known. This is called a combining problem with an *unknown change*. This structure, which is also introduced in Investigation 1, will at first be more puzzling to students than the typical unknown outcome problem. Continue to emphasize visualization of the action of the problem so that students picture clearly what they know and what they are trying to find out.

Separating In separating problems, one quantity is removed from another, resulting in a portion of the original quantity. These include "take-away" situations:

Ted had 10 marbles.
He gave 4 to Sophia.
How many does he have now?

This problem has an *unknown outcome*: We start with one quantity, that quantity is changed by removing one part, and we solve to find out what the remaining quantity is. As with combining problems, we can alter the structure of the problem by changing what information is given and what we have to find out:

Ted had 10 marbles.
He gave some to Sophia. Now he has 6.
How many did he give away?

This separating problem with an *unknown change*—how much was taken away from the initial 10 to result in an outcome of 6?—like the combining problem with an unknown change, may be more difficult for students to solve.

Continued on next page

▪ D ▪ I ▪ A ▪ L ▪ O ▪ G ▪ U ▪ E ▪ □ ▪ B ▪ O ▪ X ▪

Is It a 1 or a 10?

Two students in this class had learned the carrying and borrowing algorithms to solve problems. Other students also tried the algorithms they saw these students using. Through conversations, the teacher was able to find out what these students understood about these procedures. The following are excerpts from a discussion (p. 7) as the teacher asks three students about their approaches.

Problem: 41 – 12

[Ebony has recorded her work as shown.]

$$\begin{array}{r} 3\!\!\!\!1 \\ \cancel{4}\cancel{1} \\ -12 \\ \hline 2+9=11 \end{array}$$

Ebony: You can't take a 2 away from a 1, so you'd borrow 1 from the 4, so that's 11.

Why do you make 11 like that?

Ebony: Because it's a 10, and 10 and 1 makes 11.

OK, then what?

Ebony: So, 11 minus 2 is 9, and 3 minus 1 is 2, and then you'd put the numbers together, 2 plus 9 equals 11.

Do you think that's right?

Ebony: No, I don't think so.

Why don't you think it's right?

Ebony: Well, my other way is I counted on the 100 chart, and I went 22, 32, 42, and that was 30, and back 1 is 29.

Right now you seem to have a good method using the 100 chart, and this other method doesn't seem to make sense to you. I'd like you to use your 100 chart method for this next problem and see if you can find one other method that does make sense to you.

Ebony is trying to follow steps in a procedure from memory with little understanding of their meaning. She has trouble remembering which numbers represent multiples of 10 and which represent 1's. When she uses this procedure, she decomposes the numbers into individual digits and loses her sense of the whole quantities 41 and 12. Her other method—which she trusts more—indicates that she is working with 10's and building some understanding of how to use 10's to find the difference between two numbers. The teacher discourages her from using the borrowing algorithm.

Problem: 24 + 19

[Ping has set up his work as shown and is looking at it.]

$$\begin{array}{r} 24 \\ +19 \\ \hline \end{array}$$

Ping: Wait, do you carry the 1 or the 3? Oh, it has to be the 1 because it's 43.

You've been trying to use this method for a few days. How did you know it's 43?

Ping: Because my first way was 10 plus 20 is 30, and then I took 1 from the 4 and put it with the 9, so that's another 10, so it's 40, and I still had 3 left from the 4, so 43.

OK. You're convinced it's 43. What happens over here? [*Teacher indicates the traditional algorithm Ping has written.*]

Ping: Um . . . so 4 and 9 is 13, carry the 1 [*he writes a 3 in the ones place of the answer and carries the 1*], then 1 plus 2 plus 1— 43!

You are working hard to understand this way to do it. I want to know why you put the 3 here instead of carrying it. I know you *knew* it had to come out to 43, but I want to know if it makes sense to you.

Continued on next page

The *Investigations* curriculum incorporates the use of two forms of technology in the classroom: calculators and computers. Calculators are assumed to be standard classroom materials, available for student use in any unit. Computers are explicitly linked to one or more units at each grade level; they are used with the unit on 2-D geometry at each grade, as well as with some of the units on measuring, data, and changes.

Using Calculators

In this curriculum, calculators are considered tools for doing mathematics, similar to pattern blocks or interlocking cubes. Just as with other tools, students must learn both *how* to use calculators correctly and *when* they are appropriate to use. This knowledge is crucial for daily life, as calculators are now a standard way of handling numerical operations, both at work and at home.

Using a calculator correctly is not a simple task; it depends on a good knowledge of the four operations and of the number system, so that students can select suitable calculations and also determine what a reasonable result would be. These skills are the basis of any work with numbers, whether or not a calculator is involved.

Unfortunately, calculators are often seen as tools to check computations with, as if other methods are somehow more fallible. Students need to understand that any computational method can be used to check any other; it's just as easy to make a mistake on the calculator as it is to make a mistake on paper or with mental arithmetic. Throughout this curriculum, we encourage students to solve computation problems in more than one way in order to double-check their accuracy. We present mental arithmetic, paper-and-pencil computation, and calculators as three possible approaches.

In this curriculum we also recognize that, despite their importance, calculators are not always appropriate in mathematics instruction. Like any tools, calculators are useful for some tasks, but not for others. You will need to make decisions about when to allow students access to calculators and when to ask that they solve problems without them, so that they can concentrate on other tools and skills. At times when calculators are or are not appropriate for a particular activity, we make specific recommendations. Help your students develop their own sense of which problems they can tackle with their own reasoning and which ones might be better solved with a combination of their own reasoning and the calculator.

Managing calculators in your classroom so that they are a tool, and not a distraction, requires some planning. When calculators are first introduced, students often want to use them for everything, even problems that can be solved quite simply by other methods. However, once the novelty wears off, students are just as interested in developing their own strategies, especially when these strategies are emphasized and valued in the classroom. Over time, students will come to recognize the ease and value of solving problems mentally, with paper and pencil, or with manipulatives, while also understanding the power of the calculator to facilitate work with larger numbers.

Experience shows that if calculators are available only occasionally, students become excited and distracted when they are permitted to use them. They focus on the tool rather than on the mathematics. In order to learn when calculators are appropriate and when they are not, students must have easy access to them and use them routinely in their work.

If you have a calculator for each student, and if you think your students can accept the responsibility, you might allow them to keep their calculators with the rest of their individual materials, at least for the first few weeks of school. Alternatively, you might store them in boxes on a shelf, number each calculator, and assign a corresponding number to each student. This system can give students a sense of ownership while also helping you keep track of the calculators.

Using Computers

Students can use computers to approach and visualize mathematical situations in new ways. The computer allows students to construct and manipulate geometric shapes, see objects move according to rules they specify, and turn, flip, and repeat a pattern.

This curriculum calls for computers in units where they are a particularly effective tool for learning mathematics content. One unit on 2-D geometry at each of the grades 3–5 includes a core of activities that rely on access to computers, either in the classroom or in a lab. Other units on geometry, measurement, data, and changes include computer activities, but can be taught without them. In these units, however, students' experience is greatly enhanced by computer use.

The following list outlines the recommended use of computers in this curriculum:

Grade 1
Unit: *Survey Questions and Secret Rules*
   (Collecting and Sorting Data)
Software: Tabletop, Jr.
Source: Broderbund

Unit: *Quilt Squares and Block Towns*
   (2-D and 3-D Geometry)
Software: *Shapes*
Source: provided with the unit

Grade 2
Unit: *Mathematical Thinking at Grade 2*
   (Introduction)
Software: *Shapes*
Source: provided with the unit

Unit: *Shapes, Halves, and Symmetry*
   (Geometry and Fractions)
Software: *Shapes*
Source: provided with the unit

Unit: *How Long? How Far?* (Measuring)
Software: *Geo-Logo*
Source: provided with the unit

Grade 3
Unit: *Flips, Turns, and Area* (2-D Geometry)
Software: *Tumbling Tetrominoes*
Source: provided with the unit

Unit: *Turtle Paths* (2-D Geometry)
Software: *Geo-Logo*
Source: provided with the unit

Grade 4
Unit: *Sunken Ships and Grid Patterns*
   (2-D Geometry)
Software: *Geo-Logo*
Source: provided with the unit

Grade 5
Unit: *Picturing Polygons* (2-D Geometry)
Software: *Geo-Logo*
Source: provided with the unit

Unit: *Patterns of Change* (Tables and Graphs)
Software: *Trips*
Source: provided with the unit

Unit: *Data: Kids, Cats, and Ads* (Statistics)
Software: Tabletop, Sr.
Source: Broderbund

The software provided with the *Investigations* units uses the power of the computer to help students explore mathematical ideas and relationships that cannot be explored in the same way with physical materials. With the *Shapes* (grades 1–2) and *Tumbling Tetrominoes* (grade 3) software, students explore symmetry, pattern, rotation and reflection, area, and characteristics of 2-D shapes. With the *Geo-Logo* software (grades 3–5), students investigate rotations and reflections, coordinate geometry, the properties of 2-D shapes, and angles. The *Trips* software (grade 5) is a mathematical exploration of motion in which students run experiments and interpret data presented in graphs and tables.

We suggest that students work in pairs on the computer; this not only maximizes computer resources but also encourages students to consult, monitor, and teach one another. Generally, more than two students at one computer find it difficult to share. Managing access to computers is an issue for every classroom. The curriculum gives you explicit support for setting up a system. The units are structured on the assumption that you have enough computers for half your students to work on the machines in pairs at one time. If you do not have access to that many computers, suggestions are made for structuring class time to use the unit with five to eight computers, or even with fewer than five.

Assessment plays a critical role in teaching and learning, and it is an integral part of the *Investigations* curriculum. For a teacher using these units, assessment is an ongoing process. You observe students' discussions and explanations of their strategies on a daily basis and examine their work as it evolves. While students are busy recording and representing their work, working on projects, sharing with partners, and playing mathematical games, you have many opportunities to observe their mathematical thinking. What you learn through observation guides your decisions about how to proceed. In any of the units, you will repeatedly consider questions like these:

- Do students come up with their own strategies for solving problems, or do they expect others to tell them what to do? What do their strategies reveal about their mathematical understanding?

- Do students understand that there are different strategies for solving problems? Do they articulate their strategies and try to understand other students' strategies?

- How effectively do students use materials as tools to help with their mathematical work?

- Do students have effective ideas for keeping track of and recording their work? Does keeping track of and recording their work seem difficult for them?

You will need to develop a comfortable and efficient system for recording and keeping track of your observations. Some teachers keep a clipboard handy and jot notes on a class list or on adhesive labels that are later transferred to student files. Others keep loose-leaf notebooks with a page for each student and make weekly notes about what they have observed in class.

Assessment Tools in the Unit

With the activities in each unit, you will find questions to guide your thinking while observing the students at work. You will also find two built-in assessment tools: Teacher Checkpoints and embedded Assessment activities.

Teacher Checkpoints The designated Teacher Checkpoints in each unit offer a time to "check in" with individual students, watch them at work, and ask questions that illuminate how they are thinking.

At first it may be hard to know what to look for, hard to know what kinds of questions to ask. Students may be reluctant to talk; they may not be accustomed to having the teacher ask them about their work, or they may not know how to explain their thinking. Two important ingredients of this process are asking students open-ended questions about their work and showing genuine interest in how they are approaching the task. When students see that you are interested in their thinking and are counting on them to come up with their own ways of solving problems, they may surprise you with the depth of their understanding.

Teacher Checkpoints also give you the chance to pause in the teaching sequence and reflect on how your class is doing overall. Think about whether you need to adjust your pacing: Are most students fluent with strategies for solving a particular kind of problem? Are they just starting to formulate good strategies? Or are they still struggling with how to start? Depending on what you see as the students work, you may want to spend more time on similar problems, change some of the problems to use smaller numbers, move quickly to more challenging material, modify subsequent activities for some students, work on particular ideas with a small group, or pair students who have good strategies with those who are having more difficulty.

Embedded Assessment Activities Assessment activities embedded in each unit will help you examine specific pieces of student work, figure out what it means, and provide feedback. From the students' point of view, these assessment activities are no different from any others. Each is a learning experience in and of itself, as well as an opportunity for you to gather evidence about students' mathematical understanding.

The embedded assessment activities sometimes involve writing and reflecting; at other times, a discussion or brief interaction between student and teacher; and in still other instances, the creation and explanation of a product. In most cases, the assessments require that students *show* what they did, *write* or *talk* about it, or do both. Having to explain how they worked through a problem helps students be more focused and clear in their mathematical thinking. It also helps them realize that doing mathematics is a process that may involve tentative starts, revising one's approach, taking different paths, and working through ideas.

Teachers often find the hardest part of assessment to be interpreting their students' work. We provide guidelines to help with that interpretation. If you have used a process approach to teaching writing, the assessment in *Investigations* will seem familiar. For many of the assessment activities, a Teacher Note provides examples of student work and a commentary on what it indicates about student thinking.

Documentation of Student Growth

To form an overall picture of mathematical progress, it is important to document each student's work in journals, notebooks, or portfolios. The choice is largely a matter of personal preference; some teachers have students keep a notebook or folder for each unit, while others prefer one mathematics notebook, or a portfolio of selected work for the entire year. The final activity in each *Investigations* unit, called Choosing Student Work to Save, helps you and the students select representative samples for a record of their work.

This kind of regular documentation helps you synthesize information about each student as a mathematical learner. From different pieces of evidence, you can put together the big picture. This synthesis will be invaluable in thinking about where to go next with a particular child, deciding where more work is needed, or explaining to parents (or other teachers) how a child is doing.

If you use portfolios, you need to collect a good balance of work, yet avoid being swamped with an overwhelming amount of paper. Following are some tips for effective portfolios:

- Collect a representative sample of work, including some pieces that students themselves select for inclusion in the portfolio. There should be just a few pieces for each unit, showing different kinds of work—some assignments that involve writing, as well as some that do not.

- If students do not date their work, do so yourself so that you can reconstruct the order in which pieces were done.

- Include your reflections on the work. When you are looking back over the whole year, such comments are reminders of what seemed especially interesting about a particular piece; they can also be helpful to other teachers and to parents. Older students should be encouraged to write their own reflections about their work.

Assessment Overview

There are two places to turn for a preview of the assessment opportunities in each *Investigations* unit. The Assessment Resources column in the unit Overview Chart (pp. I-13–I-17) identifies the Teacher Checkpoints and Assessment activities embedded in each investigation, guidelines for observing the students that appear within classroom activities, and any Teacher Notes and Dialogue Boxes that explain what to look for and what types of student responses you might expect to see in your classroom. Additionally, the section About the Assessment in This Unit (p. I-21) gives you a detailed list of questions for each investigation, keyed to the mathematical emphases, to help you observe student growth.

Depending on your situation, you may want to provide additional assessment opportunities. Most of the investigations lend themselves to more frequent assessment, simply by having students do more writing and recording while they are working.

Putting Together and Taking Apart

Content of This Unit   This unit supports students in developing strategies for solving addition and subtraction problems based on an understanding of numbers, number relationships, and the operations of addition and subtraction. Students continue to work on counting with an emphasis on counting by 5's and 10's as they play games involving cubes, coins, and 100 charts. They also work with the number 100, writing equations that equal 100 and breaking 100 into multiples of 5 and 10. This work provides students with experiences that contribute to the development of addition and subtraction strategies. Throughout this unit, students solve a variety of story problems that involve combining, separating, and comparing two-digit numbers. They record and discuss their solutions.

Connections with Other Units   If you are doing the full-year *Investigations* curriculum in the suggested sequence for grade 2, this is the fifth of eight units. The work in this unit builds on the concepts and ideas that are presented in the unit *Coins, Coupons, and Combinations*. This prior unit lays some important groundwork for students developing a sense of numbers and how they are composed. In addition, their work with counting is extended in this unit as students move from counting by 1's to counting by groups. This work is important as students begin to develop their own strategies for adding and subtracting numbers.

This unit can also be successfully used at grade 3, depending on the previous experience and needs of your students.

Investigations Curriculum ■ Suggested Grade 2 Sequence

Mathematical Thinking at Grade 2 (Introduction)

Coins, Coupons, and Combinations (The Number System)

Does It Walk, Crawl, or Swim? (Sorting and Classifying Data)

Shapes, Halves, and Symmetry (Geometry and Fractions)

▶ *Putting Together and Taking Apart* (Addition and Subtraction)

How Long? How Far? (Measuring)

How Many Pockets? How Many Teeth? (Collecting and Representing Data)

Timelines and Rhythm Patterns (Representing Time)

Investigation 1 ▪ Combining and Separating

Class Sessions	Activities	Pacing
Session 1 (p. 4) INTRODUCING COMBINING SITUATIONS	Introducing the Unit Problems About Combining Sharing Strategies What's a Story for This Problem? Introducing Math Folders and Weekly Logs Homework: An Addition Story Problem	minimum 1 hr
Session 2 (p. 20) INTRODUCING SEPARATING SITUATIONS	Problems About Separating Sharing Strategies What's a Story for This Problem? Homework: A Subtraction Story Problem	minimum 1 hr
Sessions 3 and 4 (p. 28) MAKING SENSE OF ADDITION AND SUBTRACTION	Story Problems Introducing a New Type of Addition Problem Homework: Discussing Addition and Subtraction	minimum 2 hr
Sessions 5 and 6 (p. 35) WRITING STORIES FOR NUMERICAL PROBLEMS	Introducing Notation Writing Your Own Story Problems Teacher Checkpoint: Student Strategies Homework: Solving Story Problems Homework: Solving More Story Problems	minimum 2 hr
Start-Up ▪ Today's Number		

Mathematical Emphasis

- Developing models of addition and subtraction situations

- Solving problems using numerical reasoning

- Recording solution strategies clearly

- Considering the relationship between addition and subtraction

- Understanding horizontal and vertical notation for addition and subtraction

- Matching addition and subtraction notation to situations they could represent

Assessment Resources

Types of Story Problems: Combining and Separating (Teacher Note, p. 13)

How Students Learn to Add and Subtract (Teacher Note, p. 15)

What's a Story Problem? (Dialogue Box, p. 17)

Is It a 1 or a 10? (Dialogue Box, p. 18)

The Relationship Between Addition and Subtraction (Teacher Note, p. 25)

What Does It Mean to Be Finished? (Dialogue Box, p. 26)

Students' Addition and Subtraction Strategies (Teacher Note, p. 32)

Developing Numerical Strategies (Teacher Note, p. 33)

Teacher Checkpoint: Student Strategies (p. 37)

Stampeding Elephants and Other Stories (Dialogue Box, p. 39)

Materials

Counters

Student math folders

Paste or glue sticks

Family letter

Student Sheets 1–9

Teaching resource sheets

Investigation 2 ▪ Working with 100

Class Sessions	Activities	Pacing
Session 1 (p. 43) EXPLORING THE 100 CHART	What Do You Notice About the 100 Chart? Get to 100	minimum 1 hr
Session 2 (p. 49) GAMES ON THE 100 CHART	Roll-a-Square Introducing Choice Time Homework: Get to 100	minimum 1 hr
Sessions 3 and 4 (p. 59) WORKING WITH 100	Class Discussion: Moving on the 100 Chart Introducing Pinching Paper Clips Choice Time Homework: Pinching Objects	minimum 2 hr
Sessions 5 and 6 (p. 66) COLLECT $1	Collect $1 Choice Time Homework: Story Problems About 100	minimum 2 hr
Session 7 (p. 69) HOW MANY PAPER CLIPS?	Assessment: Solving a Problem About 100 Homework: Writing and Solving Story Problems 　　About 100	minimum 1 hr

Start-Up ▪ Today's Number, How Many Pockets?

Mathematical Emphasis

- Becoming familiar with the structure and patterns of the number system from 1 to 100

- Using coins as a model for adding and subtracting multiples of 5 and 10

- Using the 100 chart as a tool for combining and comparing numbers

- Developing strategies for addition and subtraction

- Comparing numbers to 100

Assessment Resources

Observing the Students (p. 47)

Observing the Students (p. 52)

Keeping Track of Students' Work (Teacher Note, p. 58)

Observing the Students (p. 63)

Moving on the 100 Chart (Dialogue Box, p. 65)

Observing the Students (p. 68)

Assessment: Solving a Problem About 100 (p. 70)

Materials

Overhead projector

Hundred Number Wall Chart

Chart markers

Number cards

Number cubes

Game pieces or markers

Counters

Interlocking cubes

Envelopes

Paper clips

Paper plates or plastic trays

Paste or glue sticks

Plastic coin sets

Paper money

Student Sheets 10–16

Teaching resource sheets

Investigation 3 ▪ Finding the Missing Part

Class Sessions	Activities	Pacing
Session 1 (p. 74) PARTS AND WHOLES	Introducing Cover-Up Class Discussion: Cover-Up Strategies	minimum 1 hr
Session 2 (p. 77) PROBLEMS WITH A MISSING PART	What Was Taken Away? More "What Was Taken Away?" Problems Homework: Cover-Up	minimum 1 hr
Sessions 3, 4, and 5 (p. 79) SEPARATING AND COMBINING CHOICES	Choice Time Teacher Checkpoint: Understanding Story Problems Class Discussion: Story Problems Homework: Find-the-Missing-Part Activities	minimum 3 hr
Start-Up ▪ Today's Number		

Mathematical Emphasis

- Developing ways to approach different sorts of addition and subtraction situations

- Recognizing and solving problem structures with a variety of givens and unknowns

- Solving problems using numerical reasoning

- Recording solution strategies clearly

- Creating situations for equations

- Comparing solution strategies

Assessment Resources

Strategies for Cover-Up (Dialogue Box, p. 76)

Observing the Students (p. 82)

Teacher Checkpoint: Understanding Story Problems (p. 83)

Materials

Overhead projector

Counters

Envelopes

Cloth pieces

Paste or glue sticks

Student Sheets 17–18

Teaching resource sheets

Investigation 4 ▪ Adding Up to 100

Class Sessions	Activities	Pacing
Session 1 (p. 88) EMMA'S ANIMALS	Ways to Make 100 A Story About 100 Equations for 100	minimum 1 hr
Session 2 (p. 96) WAYS TO MAKE 100	Class Discussion: Equations for 100 Choosing a Story and an Equation Homework: Ways to Make 100	minimum 1 hr
Sessions 3 and 4 (p. 99) STORIES ABOUT 100	Writing Stories About 100 Choice Time Sharing Stories About 100 Homework: Ways to Make $1 Extension: Sharing Stories in Other Ways	minimum 2 hr

Start-Up ▪ Today's Number, How Many Pockets?

Mathematical Emphasis

- Working with 100 and combinations of numbers that equal 100

- Adding strings of numbers by "chunking" or grouping numbers that go together

- Writing a story that reflects an addition equation

Assessment Resources

Moving from 1's to Groups (Teacher Note, p. 94)

Second Graders: A Wide Range of Students (Teacher Note, p. 95)

Ways to Make 100 (Dialogue Box, p. 98)

Stories About 100 (Teacher Note, p. 102)

Materials

Interlocking cubes

Get-to-100 recording sheets

Stuffed animals

Chart paper

Paper, lined and plain

Markers or crayons

Number cubes

Plastic coin sets

Paper money

Materials for Cover-Up (from Investigation 3)

Student Sheets 19–20

Investigation 5 ▪ Addition and Subtraction Strategies

Class Sessions	Activities	Pacing
Session 1 (p. 106) INTRODUCING COMPARING SITUATIONS	Problems About Comparing Sharing Strategies Homework: A Comparing Story Problem	minimum 1 hr
Sessions 2 and 3 (p. 112) CAPTURE 5	Introducing Capture 5 Choice Time Homework: Capture 5	minimum 2 hr
Sessions 4 and 5 (p. 118) STRATEGIES FOR COMBINING	Solving a Combining Problem The Combining Poster: Comparing Solutions Choice Time Homework: Solving Story Problems Homework: Solving More Story Problems Extension: Writing Story Problems	minimum 2 hr
Session 6 (p. 123) CAPTURE 5 STRATEGIES	Visualizing the 100 Chart Strategies for Playing Capture 5 Calculating How Far Homework: More Capture 5	minimum 1 hr
Session 7 (p. 128) STRATEGIES FOR SEPARATING	Solving a Separating Problem The Separating Poster: Comparing Solutions Choice Time Homework: Alphabet Addition	minimum 1 hr
Session 8 (p. 131) HOW FAR?	Assessment: How Far? Choosing Student Work to Save	minimum 1 hr

Start-Up ▪ Today's Number

Mathematical Emphasis

- Developing strategies for comparing two quantities

- Calculating the distance between two numbers using the 100 chart

- Developing ways to approach different types of addition and subtraction situations

- Recognizing and solving problem structures with a variety of givens and unknowns

- Solving problems using numerical reasoning

- Recording and comparing solution strategies

Assessment Resources

Observing the Students (p. 107)

Types of Story Problems: Comparing (Teacher Note, p. 109)

Counting On and Counting Back (Dialogue Box, p. 110)

Observing the Students (p. 116)

How Many Buttons? (Dialogue Box, p. 122)

Observing the Students (p. 127)

Assessment: How Far? (p. 131)

Choosing Student Work to Save (p. 132)

Assessment: How Far? (Teacher Note, p. 133)

Materials

Counters

Paste or glue sticks

Hundred Number Wall Chart

Chart markers

Number cards

Envelopes or resealable plastic bags

Markers

Game pieces

Chart paper

Index cards

Overhead projector

Student Sheets 21–29

Teaching resource sheets

Following are the basic materials needed for the activities in this unit. Many of the items can be purchased from the publisher, either individually or in the Teacher Resource Package and the Student Materials Kit for grade 2. Detailed information is available on the *Investigations* order form. To obtain this form, call toll-free 1-800-872-1100 and ask for a Dale Seymour customer service representative.

Counters such as buttons, centimeter cubes, tiles, or pennies: 45 counters per pair

Cloth scraps for covering counters (optional)

Hundred Number Wall Chart with number cards and transparent pattern markers

Snap™ Cubes (interlocking cubes): 1000

Square color tiles: about 400

Standard dot cubes (labeled 1–6 in numbers or dots): 2 per 2–3 students

Blank cubes: 2 per 2–3 students

Stickers for labeling blank cubes in multiples of 5

Plastic coin sets (real coins may be substituted), 30 pennies, 20 nickels, 20 dimes, 20 quarters: 1 set per 3–4 students

Paper money, $1 bills: at least 1 bill per student

Student math folders: 1 per student

Envelopes or resealable plastic bags for storing card sets: about 60

Paper plates or plastic trays: 1 per 2–3 students (optional)

Paper clips in boxes of 100: 10 boxes

Overhead projector (optional)

Index cards: about 100

Chart paper

Crayons or markers

Tape or pushpins

Paste or glue sticks

Paper, lined and plain

The following materials are provided at the end of this unit as blackline masters. A Student Activity Booklet containing all student sheets and teaching resources needed for individual work is available.

Family Letter (p. 147)

Student Sheets 1–29 (p. 148)

Teaching Resources:

    Story Problems, Set C (p. 157)

    Story Problems, Set E (p. 159)

    Roll-a-Square Cards (p. 167)

    Story Problems About 100 (p. 169)

    Story Problems, Set G (p. 173)

    Problem Cards (p. 175)

    Story Problems, Set H (p. 187)

    Story Problems, Set I (p. 189)

    100 Chart (p. 190)

Practice Pages (p. 191)

Related Children's Literature

Anno, Mitsumasa. *Anno's Counting House.* New York: Philomel Books, 1982.

Burningham, John. *The Shopping Basket.* New York: Thomas Y. Crowell, 1980.

Calmenson, Stephanie. *Dinner at the Panda Palace.* New York: HarperCollins, 1991.

Caple, Kathy. *The Purse.* Boston: Houghton Mifflin, 1986.

Hoban, Lillian. *Arthur's Funny Money.* New York: HarperCollins, 1981.

Lewis, Paul Owen. *You Are Cordially Invited to P. Bear's New Year's Party!* Hillsboro, Ore.: Beyond Words Publishing, 1989.

Mahy, Margaret. *The Boy Who Was Followed Home.* New York: Dial Books for Young Readers, 1975.

Mahy, Margaret. *17 Kings and 42 Elephants.* New York: Dial Books for Young Readers, 1987.

Moore, Inga. *Six-Dinner Sid.* New York: Simon and Schuster, 1991.

Russo, Marisabina. *Only Six More Days.* New York: Puffin Books, 1988.

Viorst, Judith. *Alexander Who Used to Be Rich Last Sunday.* New York: Atheneum, 1978.

Three critical parts of understanding addition and subtraction are emphasized in this unit: (1) recognizing and interpreting addition and subtraction situations; (2) choosing numerical strategies to solve the problems presented in these situations; and (3) developing knowledge about number relationships and the structure of the number system on which addition and subtraction procedures can be based.

Recognizing and interpreting addition and subtraction situations involve developing an understanding of the actions involved in these operations. For example, we can think of addition as adding two or more parts to create a new whole, and we can think of subtraction as removing a part from a whole. However, these are not the only ways to think of these operations. In this unit, students encounter situations that involve combining, separating, and comparing. Within each of these kinds of situations, they encounter a variety of problem structures. For example, here are two problems that involve separating situations:

I had 54¢ but I lost 15¢. How much money do I have left?

I had 54¢ and I lost some. Now I have 39¢. How much money did I lose?

The first problem is the familiar one of starting with a quantity, removing a part of that quantity, and finding out how much is left. The second situation also is about separating a whole into parts, but in this case we know how much we started with and how much we ended up with but don't know what quantity was removed. It is important that students learn how to visualize and describe what is happening in a problem no matter what its structure.

The second emphasis in this unit is the development of numerical strategies for solving problems. For example, for the first problem stated above, we can choose from a variety of strategies: counting up from 15, counting back from 54, adding up in groups from 15 (e.g., 15 + 5 = 20; 20 + 30 = 50; 50 + 4 = 54, so 5 + 30 + 4 = 39), subtracting in groups from 54 (e.g., 54 − 30 = 24; 24 − 4 = 20; 20 − 5 = 15), or transforming the problem (e.g., 54 − 15 is the same as 55 − 15 − 1).

Ways of visualizing the problem situation can suggest certain strategies. Mentally picturing the action of the situation as, say, a line of 54 cubes from which you break off 15 might lead to a counting backward strategy. You might think: take 1 cube off, that's 53; take 2 cubes off, that's 52; take 3 cubes off, that's 51; etc. Visualizing the 54¢ as five sticks of 10 cubes and 4 single cubes might lead to the following strategy: take away one stick of 10 and the 4 single cubes; then take away 1 more cube from one of the remaining 10's, leaving three sticks of 10 and 9 cubes. At first, students' choice of strategies may be closely connected to particular ways of seeing a problem. But as students become increasingly familiar with a variety of problem situations *and* a variety of numerical strategies, they will develop flexibility in their ability to choose strategies and apply them.

Recording our work is a critical aspect of doing mathematics, both in order to keep track of our own procedures and in order to communicate our methods and solution to others. Students are encouraged to record their work using words, numbers, and/or pictures. As part of learning to communicate mathematical relationships, they also learn to recognize and interpret standard notation for writing addition and subtraction equations. Students need to be able to look at equations such as 34 + 27 = 61 or 45 − 17 − 28 and visualize representations or situations these statements can represent.

The third emphasis of this unit is developing knowledge about number relationships and the structure of the number system. The procedures students construct to solve addition and subtraction problems must be firmly grounded in what they know about numbers and operations. Many students at this age first solve addition and subtraction problems by counting by 1's. By learning more about the number system, students learn to break numbers into manageable chunks that help them solve problems more efficiently. For example, to solve a problem like 27 + 29, one student might break each number into a multiple of 10 and some 1's and add like this: 20 + 20 = 40; 9 + 1 (from the 7) = 10; there's 6 left from the 7, so 40 + 10 + 6 = 56. Another student might think of each number as 25 plus some more and add this way: 25 + 25 + 2 + 4 = 56.

Part of becoming familiar with our number system is learning about the relationship of numbers to important landmarks in the number system, landmarks such as multiples of 10 and 100. Many of the games in the unit focus on breaking 100 into parts and on multiples of 10 and 5 as important chunks. Using 100 charts, money, and interconnecting cubes, these activities provide models of two central ideas in working with our number system: how any number is related to the nearest multiples of 10 and how any number can be broken apart into multiples of 10 and 1's (or into other parts that are easy to work with, such as 25's). Most of the addition and subtraction procedures students develop will be based on one of these two ideas.

The three emphases of this unit—interpreting problem situations, choosing appropriate numerical strategies, and using knowledge about number relationships and the number system to carry out those strategies—come together when solving a problem. What's important is that students gradually construct approaches they can rely on to solve problems accurately and efficiently and that these approaches are firmly anchored in their own developing number sense.

Mathematical Emphasis   At the beginning of each investigation, the Mathematical Emphasis section tells you what is most important for students to learn about during that investigation. Many of these understandings and processes are difficult and complex. Students gradually learn more and more about each idea over many years of schooling. Individual students will begin and end the unit with different levels of knowledge and skill, but all will gain greater knowledge about the operations of addition and subtraction.

Throughout the *Investigations* curriculum, there are many opportunities for ongoing daily assessment as you observe, listen to, and interact with students at work. In this unit, you will find two Teacher Checkpoints:

Investigation 1, Sessions 5–6:
Student Strategies (p. 37)

Investigation 3, Sessions 3–5:
Understanding Story Problems (p. 83)

This unit also has two embedded assessment activities:

Investigation 2, Session 7:
Solving a Problem About 100 (p. 70)

Investigation 5, Session 8:
How Far? (p. 131)

In addition, you can use almost any activity in this unit to assess your students' needs and strengths. Listed below are questions to help you focus your observation in each investigation. You may want to keep track of your observations for each student to help you plan your curriculum and monitor students' growth. Suggestions for documenting student growth can be found in the section About Assessment (p. I-10).

Investigation 1: Combining and Separating

■ What strategies do students have for modeling addition and subtraction problems? Are they able to visualize the action of the problem? Can they retell the problem in their own words? Do they use concrete objects? Do they seem to have mental representations of the problem?

■ Do students solve problems using numerical reasoning? Do students' strategies rely on counting by ones? Can they use strategies that count groups? Do they take numbers apart into useful chunks, manipulate these chunks, and then put them back together? How do they keep track of their number manipulations?

■ How do students record their strategies for solving problems? Can the reader understand what the child did? Do individual students rely more heavily on one method than another to record their thinking? (For example, does a student always use pictures rather than numbers or words?) Do students seem to need to talk through their strategy before recording it?

■ How aware are students of the relationships between addition and subtraction? Do they recognize when a problem can be solved with either addition or subtraction? Do students often choose to use one operation over the other, even when both would work?

■ How do students use conventional notation for recording addition and subtraction situations (+, -, =)? Are they able to interpret conventional notation and create either a mental or physical model of the problem it could represent? How familiar are students with horizontal and vertical notation? Can they interpret and sensibly solve a problem presented in either format?

■ How do students match addition and subtraction notation to problem situations? Are they able to think of a situation to go with an equation? Are they able to write an equation for a story problem?

Investigation 2: Working with 100

■ How familiar are students with the structures of the number system from 1 to 100? What patterns do they notice and how do they describe them? Are students aware of 10 as an important number in our number system?

■ How familiar are students with coins? How aware are they of the connections between coins and multiples of 5 and 10? Are they able to use coins as one model for adding and subtracting multiples of 5 and 10?

■ How do students use the 100 chart as a tool for combining and comparing numbers? What patterns do students identify on the 100 chart? Are they able to use those patterns to help them add and subtract numbers? Do students tend to move by groups when adding or subtracting on the 100 chart? by 1's?

■ What strategies are students using to solve addition and subtraction problems? Are they using groups in a meaningful way or do they count by 1's? Are they able to break apart numbers into more familiar components and then find the answer? What evidence do you see of students using 1's and 10's? Do they keep track of the context of the problem?

- How familiar are students with number combinations that make 100? What strategies do they use to figure out combinations? Do they count back from 100 by 1's? by groups? Do they count on from one number up to 100? How do their strategies vary depending on the numbers in the problem? Are their strategies changing or evolving from the strategies they used during Investigation 1? Do students use multiples of 10?

Investigation 3: Find the Missing Part

- How do students approach different types of addition and subtraction situations? Are they able to visualize the actions of different problems? Which problem types are students able to visualize and interpret easily? Do they seem to have a plan as they begin to work?

- How do students solve problems with a variety of givens and unknowns? Do they recognize that different problems have different structures? How do they solve problems in which the amount that is added or subtracted is unknown?

- Do students solve problems using numerical reasoning? Do students' strategies rely on counting by 1's? counting by groups? Do they take numbers apart into useful chunks, manipulate these chunks, and then put them back together? How do they keep track of their number manipulations?

- How clearly do students record their strategies for solving problems? Do students seem to rely more heavily on one particular method? Do they need to talk through their strategy before recording it? Has their method of recording changed over time?

- Can students create situations that match both addition and subtraction equations? Can they create problems for equations in which the part added or subtracted is unknown?

- Can students share their strategies with others clearly? Are they able to follow another student's method of solving a problem? Do they notice similarities and differences among strategies? Are they able to try someone else's strategy?

Investigation 4: Adding Up to 100

- How familiar are students with combinations of numbers that equal 100? What strategies do they use to figure combinations out? Do they count back from 100 by 1's? by groups? Do they count on from one number up to 100? How do their strategies vary depending on the numbers in the problem? Do students use multiples of 10?

- When adding strings of numbers do students look for numbers that go together easily? Do they take some numbers apart and recombine them? Do they look at the problem as a whole before they start to work? Do you see evidence of students moving from counting by 1's to counting by groups?

- How comfortable are students with writing a story that reflects adding strings of numbers that total 100? How do they keep track of all the numbers? Do they keep a running total? How do they keep track of how many more numbers they need to include in their number string?

Investigation 5: Addition and Subtraction Strategies

- What strategies do students use to compare quantities? Do they count back? Do they count on? Do they count by 1's or by groups? Do they use physical models? How do students conceptualize the problem? Do they use the 100 chart? How?

- How do students approach and visualize different sorts of addition and subtraction situations? Which problem types are students able to visualize and interpret easily? Do they seem to have a plan as they begin to work?

- How do students solve problems with a variety of givens and unknowns? Do they recognize that different problems have different structures? How do they solve problems in which the amount that is added or subtracted is unknown?

- Do students solve problems using numerical reasoning? Do students' strategies rely on counting by 1's? counting by groups? Do they take numbers apart into useful chunks, manipulate these chunks, and then put them back together? How do they keep track of their number manipulations?

■ How clearly do students record their strategies for solving problems? Do students rely more heavily on one method? For example, does a student always use pictures rather than numbers or words? Do students seem to need to talk through their strategy before recording it? Has their method of recording changed over time?

■ Can students share their strategies with others clearly? Are they able to follow another student's method of solving a problem? Do they notice similarities and differences among strategies? Are they able to try someone else's strategy?

In the *Investigations* curriculum, mathematical vocabulary is introduced naturally during the activities. We don't ask students to learn definitions of new terms; rather, they come to understand such words as *factor* or *area* or *symmetry* by hearing them used frequently in discussion as they investigate new concepts. This approach is compatible with current theories of second-language acquisition, which emphasize the use of new vocabulary in meaningful contexts while students are actively involved with objects, pictures, and physical movement.

Listed below are some key words used in this unit that will not be new to most English speakers at this age level but may be unfamiliar to students with limited English proficiency. You will want to spend additional time working on these words with your students who are learning English. If your students are working with a second-language teacher, you might enlist your colleague's aid in familiarizing students with these words before and during this unit. In the classroom, look for opportunities for students to hear and use these words. Activities you can use to present the words are given in the appendix, Vocabulary Support for Second-Language Learners (p. 144).

story Students listen to and solve a variety of story problems throughout the unit.

beginning, what happened next Students use these phrases as they visualize the actions in a story.

how far away, finish a row Students learn to move around the 100 chart, finding the distance between two numbers and how many more numbers are needed to complete a row.

Multicultural Extensions for All Students

Whenever possible, encourage students to share words, objects, customs, or any aspects of daily life from their own cultures and backgrounds that are relevant to the activities in this unit. For example:

- If you are creating your own story problems, include problems about other cultures that are familiar to your students. These problems may be about ethnic foods, clothing, currency, or special events.

- After students play the game Collect $1 in Investigation 2, ask them if they are familiar with money used in any other country. If possible, ask students to bring in any foreign currency they have to share with the class.

- As students work with 100 stories in Investigation 4, encourage them to share the name for 100 in another language. You may want to collect as many of these names as you can, having students check with family members or neighbors. Record the words children bring in on chart paper under the heading, "Ways to say 100."

Investigations

Combining and Separating

What Happens

Session 1: Introducing Combining Situations
Students solve a combining problem and record their solutions so that someone else can understand them. Strategies are shared and recorded.

Session 2: Introducing Separating Situations
Students solve a separating problem, using their own strategies. Again, they record their solutions so that someone else can understand them. As a group, students share some of their strategies while you record.

Sessions 3 and 4: Making Sense of Addition and Subtraction
Students solve a variety of story problems involving combining and separating, using their own strategies. Their job is to solve problems, check their solutions, and clearly record their approaches. Students are introduced to a new problem structure: combining with an unknown change.

Sessions 5 and 6: Writing Stories for Numerical Problems
Students write stories to fit numerical situations such as 28 + 15 or 33 − 18. They are introduced to both horizontal and vertical notation for recording addition and subtraction. They also continue to work on story problems. This is used as a Teacher Checkpoint opportunity.

Mathematical Emphasis

- Developing models of addition and subtraction situations
- Solving problems using numerical reasoning
- Recording solution strategies clearly
- Considering the relationship between addition and subtraction
- Understanding horizontal and vertical notation for addition and subtraction
- Matching addition and subtraction notation to situations they could represent

What to Plan Ahead of Time

Materials

- Counters such as interlocking cubes, color tiles, or other materials (All Sessions)
- Student math folders: 1 per student (Session 1)
- Envelopes: about 12 (Sessions 3–6)
- Paste or glue sticks (Sessions 3–6)

Other Preparation

- Duplicate student sheets and teaching resources, located at the end of this unit, in the following quantities. If you have Student Activity Booklets, copy only the item marked with an asterisk.

For Session 1
Student Sheet 1, Weekly Log (p. 148): 1 per student. At this time, you may wish to duplicate a supply to last for the entire unit and distribute the sheets as needed.

Continued on next page

What to Plan Ahead of Time *(continued)*

Family letter* (p. 147): 1 per student. Be sure to sign and date the letter before copying.

Student Sheet 2, Story Problems, Set A (p. 149) or copies of problems you have created: 1 per student

Student Sheet 3, An Addition Story Problem (p. 150): 1 per student (homework)

For Session 2

Student Sheet 4, Story Problems, Set B (p. 151) or copies of problems you have created: 1 per student

Student Sheet 5, A Subtraction Story Problem (p. 152): 1 per student (homework)

For Sessions 3–4

Story Problems, Set C (p. 157) or copies of problems you have created. 1 per student and 1 extra. Cut the sheets apart into individual problems. Store the copies of each problem in a separate envelope. Paste an example of each problem on the front of the envelope so students can see which problem they are choosing.

Student Sheet 6, Story Problems, Set D (p. 153) or copies of problems you have created: 1 per student

Student Sheet 7, Discussing Addition and Subtraction (p. 154): 1 per student (homework)

For Sessions 5–6

Story Problems, Set E (p. 159) or copies of problems you have created: 1 per student.

Cut apart into individual problems. Store copies of each problem in a separate envelope.

Student Sheet 8, Problem Strategies (p. 155): 2 per student (homework)

Student Sheet 9, Writing and Solving a Story Problem (p. 156): 1 per student (homework)

■ Think about situations familiar to students that you might use as contexts for addition and subtraction problems. Throughout this unit, you may want to substitute problems of your own. For more information, see the **Teacher Note**, Creating Your Own Story Problems (p. 11). If you use your own problem contexts, create the following kinds of problems: a combining problem (with follow-up) for Session 1, a separating problem (with follow-up) for Session 2, a mixture of 6–8 problems for Sessions 3 and 4 (combining and separating with unknown outcomes) a combining problem with unknown change (with follow-up) for Session 4, and two combining problems with unknown change (with follow-ups) for Sessions 5 and 6. See the **Teacher Note**, Types of Story Problems: Combining and Separating (p. 13) for more information about problem types.

■ Prepare a math folder for each student, if this was not done for a previous unit. (Session 1)

Introducing Combining Situations

Materials

- Counters
- Student Sheet 1 (1 per student)
- Student Sheet 2 (1 per student)
- Family letter (1 per student)
- Student math folders (1 per student)
- Student Sheet 3 (1 per student, homework)

What Happens

Students solve a combining problem and record their solutions so that someone else can understand them. Strategies are shared and recorded. Their work focuses on:

- visualizing combining situations
- developing strategies for combining
- recording strategies clearly

Start-Up

Today's Number   Today's Number is one of three routines that are built into the grade 2 *Investigations* curriculum. Routines provide students regular practice in important mathematical ideas such as number combinations, counting and estimating data, and concepts of time. For Today's Number, which is done daily (or most days), students write number sentences that equal the number of days they have been in school. The complete description of Today's Number (pp. 135–137) offers suggestions for establishing this routine and some variations.

If you are doing the full-year grade 2 *Investigations* curriculum, you will have already started a 200 chart and a counting strip during the unit *Mathematical Thinking at Grade 2*. Write the next number on the 200 chart and add the next number card to the counting strip. As a class, brainstorm ways to express the number.

If you are teaching an *Investigations* unit for the first time, here are a few options for incorporating Today's Number as a routine:

- **Begin with 1**   Begin a counting line that does not correspond to the school day number. Each day add a number to the strip and use this number as Today's Number.
- **Use the Calendar Date**   If today is the sixteenth day of the month, use 16 as Today's Number.

After Today's Number has been established, ask students to think about different ways to write the number. Post a piece of chart paper to record their suggestions. You might want to offer ideas to help students get started. If Today's Number is 45, you might suggest 40 + 5 or 20 + 25.

Ask students to think about other ways to make Today's Number. List their suggestions on chart paper. As students offer suggestions, occasionally ask the group if they agree with the statements. This gives students the opportunity to confirm an idea that they might have had or to respond to an incorrect suggestion.

As students grow accustomed to this routine, they will begin to see patterns in the combinations, have favorite kinds of number sentences, or use more complicated types of expressions. Today's Number can be recorded daily on Student Sheet 1, Weekly Log. (See p. 9.)

Activity

Introducing the Unit

Introduce the unit by telling students that during the next few weeks they will be working on addition and subtraction. Students will solve story problems, work with the 100 chart, and play some new games. To get a sense of what students already know, ask questions such as, "Who can tell us something about addition?" "What do you think about when I say subtraction?" "What is a story problem?" See the **Dialogue Box,** What's a Story Problem? (p. 17), to see how one teacher introduced the unit.

Activity

Problems About Combining

Introduce a problem such as the one below to the whole class. You may want to put the problem in a context more familiar to your students. See the **Teacher Note,** Creating Your Own Story Problems (p. 11).

I am going to read you a story problem and I would like you to solve it in a way that makes sense to you. You can use interlocking cubes, color tiles, or any materials you want to. Your job is not only to solve the problem but also to write about what you do using words, pictures, and/or numbers so that someone else can understand it. After everyone has finished, we'll share the strategies we used to solve the problem.

Read the following problem aloud.

A class of 29 students is going on a trip to the science museum. There are 12 adults going with them. How many people are going on the trip?

Before students begin work, make sure they understand what the problem is asking. It can be very useful for students to visualize a problem. To help them with this process, ask students to do one or more of the following:

- act out the problem
- close their eyes and imagine the action, then describe how they saw it
- tell the problem in their own words

Close your eyes while I read the problem again. Imagine that you are watching what is happening. [*Reread the problem.*] Do you see the students and the adults? Tell me about what you see. Do you think the answer will be more than 29 or less than 29? Why?

Provide each student with Student Sheet 2, Story Problems, Set A (or other problems if you are creating your own contexts). You may want to have a container of cubes or other materials available for students to use.

Students should work individually on problem 1, but seat them in groups so they can discuss their strategies. Remind them that they are to solve the problem and use words, pictures, and/or numbers to record their strategy. The **Dialogue Box**, What Does It Mean to Be Finished? (p. 26), shows how one teacher worked with students to help them record their work.

You may see a variety of approaches as you observe students working. Students may *count all* by counting out two piles of objects, putting them together, then counting the whole pile beginning with 1, *count on* by beginning with one quantity and counting up, or use numerical reasoning strategies such as separating 10's and 1's or counting on by 10's.

Throughout this investigation, the algorithms (procedures) for "carrying" and "borrowing" are likely to come up if students have learned these procedures elsewhere. When students offer these approaches in class, it's important that their methods are accepted. However, as is expected of all students, they must be able to justify and explain these procedures. For more information about why it is important for students to develop their own procedures and how to handle carrying and borrowing, see the **Teacher Note**, How Students Learn to Add and Subtract (p. 15) and the **Dialogue Box**, Is It a 1 or a 10? (p. 18).

As you observe students working, encourage them to describe their strategies clearly. You may need to tell students to revise what they have written or drawn. Students who solve this problem easily and record their strategies clearly can find a way to double-check their answer. Students who are counting all or counting on should find ways to double-check their counting. It is very easy for any of us to miscount; students need to find ways to be sure they are counting accurately.

If you find the numbers in the problem are too large for some students, modify the problem to use smaller numbers. If some students finish easily, have them try the same problem again with larger numbers.

When students are finished, they can describe their solutions to partners. Students who have time can work on Student Sheet 2, problem 2, recording their strategies below the problem.

Notice the variety of approaches students use, so that you can encourage those with different strategies to share their work with the class in the next part of the session.

Sharing Strategies

The whole group meets together to share strategies. Have something to count with available for students to demonstrate counting-all or counting-on strategies. As students share strategies, record them on the chalkboard. The ways you record will give students models for recording their own work. Number the strategies so students can refer to them easily ("Mine is like the first way," "Mine is almost the same as the second way, but . . ."). It's probably not wise to label them with students' names because other students are likely to have approached the problem in similar ways, and all students will enjoy feeling ownership of a strategy.

Here are the ways one teacher recorded six different approaches:

29 + 12

1. 30 31 32 33 34 35 36 37 38 39 40 41
    1 2 3 4 5 6 7 8 9 10 11 12
   Started at 30 and counted up 12. Counted the numbers to be sure it shows adding 12.

2. 20 + 10 = 30
   9 + 2 = 11
   30 + 10 = 40
   40 + 1 = 41

3. 29 + 10 = 39
   39 + 2 = 41

4. 29 + 2 = 31
   31 + 10 = 41

5. OOOOOOOOOOOOOOOOOOOOOOOOOOOOOOOO
   OOOOOOOOOOO
   Drew circles and counted all.

6. 29 + 1 = 30
   30 + 11 = 41
   Took 1 away from 12 and added it to 29 to get 30. Added on 11.

After a student has shared a strategy, ask:

Did anyone have a way that is similar to this one? Did anyone have a way that is different from the way(s) written here?

Encourage students to elaborate if they say their way is almost the same.

Before discussion ends, ask each student to look at his or her own strategy and decide which of the ones you've recorded is closest to it. Ask students to raise hands to show which strategy they used. This is a way of validating all students' work and of giving you a sense of what kinds of strategies are being used in your class as a whole.

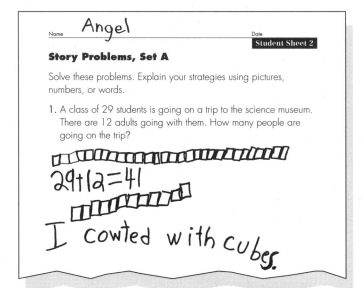

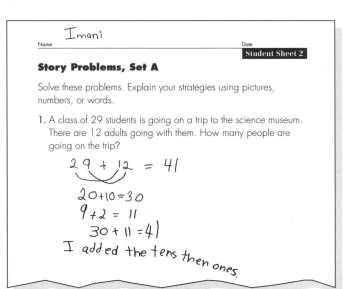

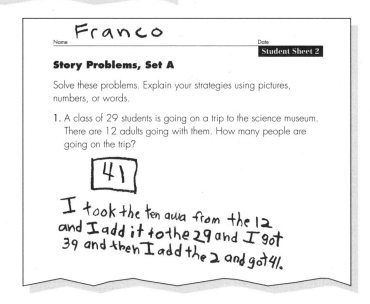

Write an addition expression on the chalkboard and ask students to think of a story for it. For example, write 11 + 13.

Look at what I have written. Who can think of a story problem for 11 plus 13?

You may need to give an example to help get students started. After several story problems have been suggested, end the session by having each student write a story problem for another addition expression that you provide.

If you are using the full-year *Investigations* curriculum, students will be familiar with math folders and Weekly Logs. If this curriculum is new to students, tell them about one way they will keep track of their math work.

Mathematicians show how they think about and solve problems by talking about their work, drawing pictures, building models, and explaining their work in writing so that they can share their ideas with other people. Your math folder will be a place to collect the writing and drawing that you do in math class.

Distribute math folders to students and have them label the folders with their names.

Your math folder is a place to keep track of what you do each day in math class. Sometimes there will be more than one activity to choose from, and at other times, like today, everyone in the class will do the same thing. Each day you will record what you did on this Weekly Log.

Distribute Student Sheet 1, Weekly Log, and ask students to write their names at the top of the page. Point out that there are spaces for each day of the week and ask them to write today's date on the line after the appropriate day. If you are doing the activity Today's Number, students can write the number in the box beside the date.

Ask students for suggestions about what to call today's activities. Titles for choices and whole-class activities should be short, to encourage all students to record what they do each day. List their ideas on the board and let students choose one title to write in the space below the date.

❖ **Tip for the Linguistically Diverse Classroom** Encourage students who are not writing comfortably in English to use drawings to record in their Weekly Log. If students demonstrate some proficiency in writing, suggest that they record a few words with their drawings. Students can also record a sample problem representative of each day's work.

Weekly Logs can be stapled to the front of the folders (each new week on the top so prior logs can be viewed by lifting up the sheets).

During the unit (or throughout the year), you might use the math folders and Weekly Logs in a number of ways:

■ to keep track of what kinds of activities students choose to do and how frequently they choose them

■ to review with students, individually or as a group, the work they've accomplished

■ to share student work with families, either by sending folders home periodically for students to share, or during student/family/teacher conferences

Session 1 Follow-Up

 **Homework**

An Addition Story Problem Have students write and solve a word problem that's about combining two things, using something that they can see out their windows at home. Again, they need to show their solution strategy with some combination of numbers, words, and pictures on Student Sheet 3.

Send home the family letter (p. 147) or the *Investigations* at Home booklet.

Creating Your Own Story Problems ⟩ Teacher Note

Throughout this unit, students will be meeting addition and subtraction situations. You may want to use the story problems in this unit or you may want to create your own problems. Creating your own problems enables you to use contexts that reflect the interest, knowledge, and experience of your students. You may also want to adjust the numbers in the problems for different students in your class. The following provides information about developing appropriate problems.

Important Note   It is important that you provide a variety of problem structures for each student. If you change the contexts or numbers in a problem, try not to alter the structure of the problem. See the **Teacher Notes**, Types of Story Problems (p. 13 and p. 109), for more information about this aspect of creating problems.

Creating Interesting Contexts   In creating addition and subtraction situations, use contexts that are familiar and interesting to students without being distracting. For example, the first problem in the unit (see Student Sheet 2) is about a trip to a science museum. Your students may not have any experience with what a science museum is, so you can easily change the problem to be about a trip to a familiar place in your own community.

Simple, familiar situations may be the most satisfying. One source of good situations is experiences that all students have had. For example, one urban class walks to a nearby park every day for recess; a problem based on that experience might be:

Last Thursday at the park, I counted 29 squirrels on the ground and 12 more in the trees. How many squirrels were in the park?

Another class is having a series of bake sales at lunchtime to raise money for a class trip:

Last Friday we sold 29 chocolate cupcakes and 12 vanilla cupcakes. How many cupcakes did we sell?

In one classroom, the teacher made up two characters, Ted and Sophia, who had experiences very much like those of her students, and built problem situations around these characters:

Ted and Sophia got a bag of peanuts. On the way home, Ted ate 29 peanuts and Sophia ate 12 peanuts. How many peanuts did they eat?

Sophia and Ted went to the post office. Sophia bought 29 stamps and Ted bought 12 stamps. How many stamps did they have?

Many teachers also take advantage of special events, classroom happenings, seasons, or holidays for problem contexts:

If Ebony made 29 snowballs and Tim made 12, how many snowballs did they have?

Follow-up Problems   Simple, familiar situations often suggest other problems that easily follow from the initial problem. These problems can be posed for students who have finished the first problem. Additional questions related to the examples given above might include:

In the park on Friday, I counted 26 squirrels on the ground and 14 in the trees. Did I see more, fewer, or the same number of squirrels on Friday than I saw on Thursday?

How many more chocolate cupcakes did we sell than vanilla cupcakes?

We had 50 cupcakes altogether. How many were not sold?

If we charge 10¢ for each cupcake, how much will we get for all the cupcakes?

The next Friday we sold twice as many cupcakes. How many cupcakes did we sell?

If Ebony and Tim want to have 60 snowballs, how many more snowballs do they need to make?

Continued on next page

In creating follow-up problems, consider whether to keep the level of challenge about the same or to make the problem easier or more difficult. See the **Teacher Notes**, Types of Story Problems (p. 13 and p. 109), for more information about the relative difficulty of different problem structures.

Adjusting Numbers in the Problem   You may have students who are comfortable working with numbers in the 20's, 30's, 40's, and higher, and other students who need to work with smaller numbers. Students who are primarily using counting strategies may lose track if the numbers with which they're working are too high.

Start with the numbers suggested for each problem and then adjust the numbers after students have solved the basic problem. In this way both you and students have some immediate information about the level of difficulty of the problem. Sometimes you can choose the new numbers. At other times, let students choose appropriate numbers for themselves from some you suggest. Ask students to choose numbers that make the problem a little difficult for them. Let them know that different numbers will be challenging for different students and that it's important for each student to work with problems that are right for him or her.

Students at this age are often fascinated with larger numbers and may choose numbers that are too difficult for them. When their energy is focused on working with large numbers, they easily lose track of the problem situation and their own strategies. Encourage students to work with numbers that make sense for them.

Types of Story Problems: Combining and Separating

In the elementary grades, students are often exposed to only a few types of story problems. The two problem types that are most familiar are addition of two quantities to find a total and subtraction in which one quantity is removed from another.

Current research has focused on how students in the primary grades solve addition and subtraction problems. One outcome of this research has been to identify the variety of problem types that students should encounter in the elementary grades. Students usually do not encounter a wide enough variety of problem structures and therefore have a limited idea of how to apply addition and subtraction to solve problems.

In this unit, students will encounter three basic problem structures—combining, separating, and comparing. This note describes combining and separating, which are introduced in Investigations 1 and 3. Comparing situations will be introduced in Investigation 5 and are discussed in the **Teacher Note,** Types of Story Problems: Comparing (p. 109).

Combining These are problems in which two quantities are combined to form a third quantity. Called *joining* or *combining* problems, these include familiar addition situations such as:

> Ted had 6 marbles.
> Sophia gave him 4 more.
> How many does Ted have now?

In this combining situation, the two quantities to be combined are known, and their sum is to be found. These are problems with an *unknown outcome*—the parts are combined and the outcome of that combining action, the total, is unknown. However, it is also important that students encounter combining situations in which the whole and one quantity are known and the second quantity must be found:

> Ted had 6 marbles. Sophia gave him some.
> Now Ted has 10 marbles.
> How many did Sophia give him?

How the problem is solved is not what determines whether this is a combining problem. Some students might solve it by subtracting 6 from 10; others might think of it as, "What do I need to add to 6 to get 10?" However it is solved, the structure is considered combining—two quantities are combined to create a third. In this case the *outcome* is known, but the *change* that occurs—what was added to 6—is not known. This is called a combining problem with an *unknown change*. This structure, which is also introduced in Investigation 1, will at first be more puzzling to students than the typical unknown outcome problem. Continue to emphasize visualization of the action of the problem so that students picture clearly what they know and what they are trying to find out.

Separating In separating problems, one quantity is removed from another, resulting in a portion of the original quantity. These include "take-away" situations:

> Ted had 10 marbles.
> He gave 4 to Sophia.
> How many does he have now?

This problem has an *unknown outcome*: We start with one quantity, that quantity is changed by removing one part, and we solve to find out what the remaining quantity is. As with combining problems, we can alter the structure of the problem by changing what information is given and what we have to find out:

> Ted had 10 marbles.
> He gave some to Sophia. Now he has 6.
> How many did he give away?

This separating problem with an *unknown change*—how much was taken away from the initial 10 to result in an outcome of 6?—like the combining problem with an unknown change, may be more difficult for students to solve.

Continued on next page

However, with increased familiarity, they will more easily solve problems that ask them to find the change rather than the outcome. This problem type is introduced in Investigation 3.

To summarize, the types of combining and separating problems students will encounter in this unit are shown in the chart below.

Note: There are more distinctions in research among problem types than have been included here. In fact, different researchers have sorted problems in different ways. For example, some researchers have a special category called *part-part-whole* for problems such as this one.

> There are 10 people coming to my party.
> 6 of them are girls.
> How many are boys?

In this problem, there is no combining or separating *action*, but the problem is very similar in structure to a combining or separating problem. The information given here will provide you with a good beginning in creating problems with a variety of structures for students.

	Unknown Outcome	**Unknown Change**
Combining	6 marbles and 5 marbles <u>unknown total</u>	6 marbles and <u>some added</u> 11 total
Separating	11 marbles, 5 taken away <u>unknown amount left</u>	11 marbles, <u>some taken away</u> 6 left

How Students Learn to Add and Subtract

For many years students were taught to add and subtract using only a particular algorithm (procedure). To add, they were taught to "carry," and to subtract, they were taught to "borrow." Researchers and educators have found that most students learn these algorithms without connecting them to the meaning of the numbers and the structure of the problem. The carrying and borrowing procedures focus attention on individual digits in the numbers rather than on the whole quantities and their relationships. When encouraged to develop their own strategies based on sound number sense, students are able to develop procedures that are mathematically sound, efficient, and can be generalized to any problem. Students feel a sense of ownership for an approach when they construct it themselves based on what they understand about the number system and number relationships.

We want students to be able to solve computation problems efficiently and accurately. This unit helps students develop the number sense necessary to be able to solve numerical problems in whatever contexts they appear. There are many algorithms that, while both efficient and accurate, also keep more visible the connections between the numbers and the problem situation. In this unit, students develop such procedures, which are connected closely to the meaning of the operations and are based on number relationships they know.

What are the goals for students as they develop procedures to solve addition and subtraction problems? Speed should not be a criterion for solving any kind of mathematics problem. Rather, *efficiency in use* is the critical criterion for students' mastery of computation with whole numbers. Let's look at an example. Suppose you want to add 65 and 28. One way you might do this is to think of this problem as 60 + 20 + 5 + 5 + 3. If you know how to add multiples of 10 and recognize that 5 + 5 is also equal to 10, you can easily arrive at the solution of 93. This method is as efficient as the "carrying" algorithm, is easy to keep track of, results in numbers that are easy to work with, and takes seconds to carry out.

The most important criterion for student-developed strategies is that they are based on sound number sense and understanding of the problem. Solving the problem in the way shown above requires knowledge of how a two-digit number is composed of a multiple of 10 and 1's and how numbers can be taken apart and recombined in any order in an addition problem.

While we are not aiming for speed, we do need strategies that allow us to solve computation problems in ways that are efficient. For example, some students might solve this problem by starting at 65 and counting on 28 ones (66, 67, 68, 69, . . . 93). These students have developed a mental model of the meaning of 65 + 28; this method, if carried out accurately, will give a correct solution. However, counting by 1's becomes unmanageable and is prone to errors as numbers get larger. Students need to develop an understanding about how these numbers are composed which will lead to more efficient approaches. Efficiency requires the chunking of numbers in an addition or subtraction problem into groups (such as breaking numbers into 10's and 1's) so that they are easier to work with. You will notice that the students in your class develop a variety of different procedures and that individual students use different procedures for different problem types.

The procedures that students develop in the primary grades will eventually be applied to larger problems. For example, one of the program authors solves a problem like 1573 + 1684 + 328 as follows:

1000 + 1000 + 500 + 600 + 300 + 70 + 80 + 20 + 3 + 4 + 8 =

She adds the sum of the multiples of 1000 and 100 (3400), the sum of the multiples of 10 (170) and the sum of the 1's (15). 3400 + 170 + 15 = 3585.

Continued on next page

Approaches like this one, based on sound number sense and knowledge of our base-ten number system, are efficient and accurate for solving virtually any problem we would reasonably encounter in life.

It is likely that the historically taught carrying and borrowing algorithms will appear in your classroom, whether or not you introduce them. Students may have learned them in a previous grade or may learn them at home. Treat this algorithm like any other procedure students use—as a strategy that students must be able to explain and justify. See the **Dialogue Box**, Is It a 1 or a 10? (p. 18), for an example of how one teacher worked with students who were using these algorithms.

Use the following guidelines:

■ Encourage all students who use a single approach, including those students who use the historically taught algorithms, to develop more than one approach to solving addition and subtraction problems. Having more than one approach allows students to be flexible in matching strategies to problems and to check one strategy by using another.

■ Work with students who know the carrying and borrowing algorithms to see if they know how their shortcut notation relates to what is going on in the problem. If they can recite the steps but do not know how those steps relate to what they are trying to find out, or if they frequently lose track of the procedure, discourage them from using these procedures.

DIALOGUE BOX

What's a Story Problem?

As this class begins the unit (p. 5), the teacher tries to get a sense of what kinds of problems students have encountered previously.

We're going to solve story problems. Who can tell us what a story problem is?

Tory: They're problems like Sally and Kim went to the beach. Sally collected 20 shells, Kim collected 5, how much altogether?

OK. Can someone tell me how they might solve that problem?

Angel: 20 and then add on 5.

Why?

Angel: Because Kim collected 5.

OK. But how would you do it?

Ayaz: I've memorized it in my head. It's like 20, then 5 . . . 25. The word gives you the answer.

Camilla: I counted.

How did you count? [*Student doesn't answer.*] **Do you mean like 21, 22, . . . ?** [*Camilla nods.*]

Graham: Since you have 5 fingers, you just count each finger.

This is one example of a story problem. Does someone have a different kind?

Bjorn: On Valentine's day, Talia got 55 cards and Tim got 32 cards. How many more cards did Talia get than Tim? It's subtraction.

You would want to subtract. Someone else might solve it a different way.

Lionel: If you're adding 20 and 11, you can't just say "twenty-eleven." You have to do it another way.

Oh, you're going back to what Ayaz said about 25?

Lionel: Yeah.

Through this kind of open-ended conversation, the teacher does some initial assessment. The teacher notes, for example, Camilla's reluctance to describe a strategy out loud and Bjorn's use of a problem with a comparison structure rather than the more common take-away structure to illustrate subtraction. The teacher recognizes the potential opening here for some discussion of the relationship between addition and subtraction—either of which might be used to solve the comparison problem—as something to come back to later in the unit.

Two students in this class had learned the carrying and borrowing algorithms to solve problems. Other students also tried the algorithms they saw these students using. Through conversations, the teacher was able to find out what these students understood about these procedures. The following are excerpts from a discussion (p. 7) as the teacher asks three students about their approaches.

Problem: 41 – 12

[*Ebony has recorded her work as shown.*]

$$\overset{3}{\cancel{4}}\,\overset{1}{\cancel{1}}$$
$$-1\,2$$
$$2+9 = 11$$

Ebony: You can't take a 2 away from a 1, so you'd borrow 1 from the 4, so that's 11.

Why do you make 11 like that?

Ebony: Because it's a 10, and 10 and 1 makes 11.

OK, then what?

Ebony: So, 11 minus 2 is 9, and 3 minus 1 is 2, and then you'd put the numbers together, 2 plus 9 equals 11.

Do you think that's right?

Ebony: No, I don't think so.

Why don't you think it's right?

Ebony: Well, my other way is I counted on the 100 chart, and I went 22, 32, 42, and that was 30, and back 1 is 29.

Right now you seem to have a good method using the 100 chart, and this other method doesn't seem to make sense to you. I'd like you to use your 100 chart method for this next problem and see if you can find one other method that does make sense to you.

Ebony is trying to follow steps in a procedure from memory with little understanding of their meaning. She has trouble remembering which numbers represent multiples of 10 and which represent 1's. When she uses this procedure, she decomposes the numbers into individual digits and loses her sense of the whole quantities 41 and 12. Her other method—which she trusts more—indicates that she is working with 10's and building some understanding of how to use 10's to find the difference between two numbers. The teacher discourages her from using the borrowing algorithm.

Problem: 24 + 19

[*Ping has set up his work as shown and is looking at it.*]

$$24$$
$$+\underline{19}$$

Ping: Wait, do you carry the 1 or the 3? Oh, it has to be the 1 because it's 43.

You've been trying to use this method for a few days. How did you know it's 43?

Ping: Because my first way was 10 plus 20 is 30 and then I took 1 from the 4 and put it with the 9, so that's another 10, so it's 40, and I still had 3 left from the 4, so 43.

OK. You're convinced it's 43. What happens over here? [*Teacher indicates the traditional algorithm Ping has written.*]

Ping: Um . . . so 4 and 9 is 13, carry the 1 [*he writes a 3 in the ones place of the answer and carries the 1*], then 1 plus 2 plus 1— 43!

You are working hard to understand this way to do it. I want to know why you put the 3 here instead of carrying it. I know you *knew* it had to come out to 43, but I want to know if it makes sense to you.

Continued on next page

continued

Ping: Because the 3 is in the 13, it's like the ones part, you just have to leave it there so it will be the end part of the number.

Ping has a strong approach to addition based on his understanding of how to take apart numbers and recombine them, and he uses those ideas to guide his experimentation with "carrying." As long as he continues to relate his use of carrying to his own algorithms, his teacher will not worry about his use of the carrying notation. The teacher will monitor Ping to be sure he continues to make sense of the numbers in a problem.

Problem: 24 + 19

[Rosie has set up her problem vertically and solved it using the carrying notation.]

What's this 1 [*teacher points to the "carried" 1*]? **How come you put it there?**

Rosie: This place [*points to the ones place*] is like 1, 2, 3, 4. This [*points to the tens place*] is like all the numbers from 10 to 99.

So you could have an 11 here [*in the tens place*]?

Rosie: No, it's just 10, 20, 30, 40.

It worries me how the 1 becomes a 10.

Rosie: I know. It's from the 13. It's 1, but it stands for 10. So I did 4 plus 9 equals 13, carry the 1, then 1 plus 2 plus 1.

Can you explain the 1 plus 2 plus 1?

Rosie: 10 plus 20 plus 10 is 40, so it's 43.

Rosie is articulating important ideas about values of numerals in the ones place and the tens place. She has grasped the idea that the 13 can be split into a 3 and a 10 and that her carried 1 actually represents a 10. The teacher will continue to urge her to develop other methods as

well and be sure that she can make sense of what the numbers mean when she chooses to use this method.

Note: The teacher carefully listens to all strategies and doesn't reject the carrying or borrowing algorithm when it comes from the students. However, just as students are to explain and justify any other approach, they are expected to explain and justify this one. The difference between this method and others that students are using is that this one is usually not constructed by students as they make sense of numbers and operations but is learned as a procedure apart from the meaning of the numbers and operations. Therefore, the teacher is especially careful in checking with students who are using carrying and borrowing procedures and notation.

Introducing Separating Situations

Materials

- Counters
- Student Sheet 4 (1 per student)
- Student Sheet 5 (1 per student, homework)

What Happens

Students solve a separating problem, using their own strategies. Again, they record their solutions so that someone else can understand them. As a group, students share some of their strategies while you record. Their work focuses on:

- visualizing separating situations
- developing strategies for separating
- recording strategies clearly

Start-Up

Combining Problem   Ask students about their experience writing problems for homework. You may choose to collect students' work and look at their problems to give you a sense of whether students were able to create a combining situation that matched an addition expression.

Today's Number

- **Calendar Date**   If you are using the calendar date for Today's Number, brainstorm with students ways to express the number. Record students' expressions on chart paper so that they can be saved each day.
- **Number of School Days**   If you are using the number of school days as Today's Number, and the number is over 100, encourage students to break the number into parts such as 100 + 10, then offer suggestions for how to express one of those numbers, keeping the other intact. For example: 100 + 5 + 5 or 100 + 4 + 4 + 2. Add a card to the class counting strip and fill in another number on the blank 200 chart.

Problems About Separating

This session focuses on separating situations and is parallel to Session 1, Introducing Combining Situations. Introduce a problem such as the one below to the whole class. As in Session 1, you may want to change the context of the problem so that it is more familiar to students. Keep the same numbers and the basic structure of the problem. The **Teacher Notes**, Creating Your Own Story Problems (p. 11) and Types of Story Problems: Combining and Separating (p. 13), provide help for developing your own problems.

If you are using the story problems on the student sheets, help students visualize the first problem on Student Sheet 4. If you are using your own problems, read one aloud.

Close your eyes and imagine what is happening in this story problem. Yesterday at the park, I counted 39 pigeons. When a big dog walked by, 17 of them flew away. How many were still there?

Do you think the answer to this problem will be more or fewer than 39 pigeons? Why?

Provide each student with Student Sheet 4, Story Problems, Set B. Explain that you would like students to solve the problem in a way that makes sense to them and record their strategies so that someone else can understand what they did. As you observe students working, remind them to be clear as they describe their strategies. See the **Dialogue Box**, What Does It Mean to Be Finished? (p. 26), for examples of how teachers helped students revise and expand their attempts at recording their work.

❖ **Tip for the Linguistically Diverse Classroom** While students with limited English proficiency can make use of drawings and numbers to show most of their thinking behind their strategies, they may be limited in their ability to write sentences that articulate what they did (for example, "I used blocks," "I counted on my fingers"). As a class, brainstorm a list of possible strategies and create a rebus for each one.

count on fingers   use cubes   draw a picture

Students with limited English proficiency can incorporate ideas from the strategy list when writing their responses. Keep this list available for students throughout the unit.

Have counting materials available for those who want to use them. Students can work individually or in pairs, but each student records individually.

Students who have time can do problem 2 on Student Sheet 4.

Sharing Strategies

Meet together as a whole class to share solution strategies for this problem. Again, use this time as an opportunity to model ways of recording a variety of solutions. The following solutions were offered in one classroom.

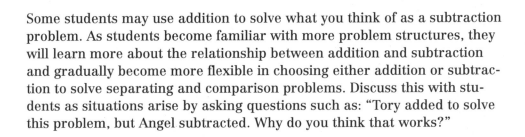

39 – 17

1. OOOOOOOOOOOOOOOOOOOOOOOOOOOOOOOOO
OOOOOOOOOOOOOOO
Counted out 39, then crossed out 17. Counted what was left.

2. Counted backward: 38, 37, 36, 35, 34, 33, 32, 31, 30, 29, 28, 27, 26, 25, 24, 23, 22

3. $30 - 10 = 20$
$9 - 7 = 2$
$20 + 2 = 22$

4. $39 - 10 = 29$
$29 - 7 = 22$

5. $17 + 3 = 20$
$20 + 10 = 30$
$30 + 9 = 39$
$3 + 10 + 9 = 22$

6. Counted on the number line.
Started at 18 and counted up to 39.
Got 22.

Some students may use addition to solve what you think of as a subtraction problem. As students become familiar with more problem structures, they will learn more about the relationship between addition and subtraction and gradually become more flexible in choosing either addition or subtraction to solve separating and comparison problems. Discuss this with students as situations arise by asking questions such as: "Tory added to solve this problem, but Angel subtracted. Why do you think that works?"

See the **Teacher Note**, The Relationship Between Addition and Subtraction (p. 25), for more information on the important connections between these two operations.

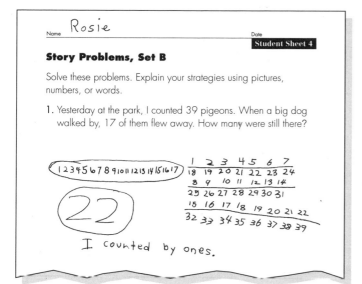

Name _Rosie_   Date _____
Student Sheet 4

Story Problems, Set B

Solve these problems. Explain your strategies using pictures, numbers, or words.

1. Yesterday at the park, I counted 39 pigeons. When a big dog walked by, 17 of them flew away. How many were still there?

I counted by ones.

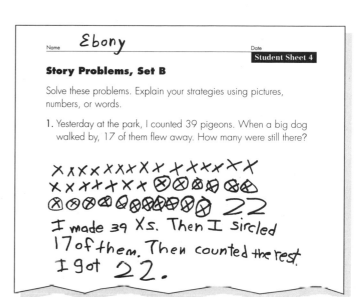

Name _Ebony_   Date _____
Student Sheet 4

Story Problems, Set B

Solve these problems. Explain your strategies using pictures, numbers, or words.

1. Yesterday at the park, I counted 39 pigeons. When a big dog walked by, 17 of them flew away. How many were still there?

I made 39 Xs. Then I sircled 17 of them. Then counted the rest. I got 22.

Name _Graham_   Date _____
Student Sheet 4

Story Problems, Set B

Solve these problems. Explain your strategies using pictures, numbers, or words.

1. Yesterday at the park, I counted 39 pigeons. When a big dog walked by, 17 of them flew away. How many were still there?

$$39 - 17$$
$$20 + 2 = 22$$

I took away tens. Then I took away 1 s.

What's a Story for This Problem?

As you have recorded students' strategies, you have been modeling addition and subtraction notation. You can also help students connect subtraction notation with situations it might represent by writing a subtraction expression on the chalkboard and asking students to create a story problem for it. Write 18 – 12 on the chalkboard.

Who can think of a story problem for 18 – 12?

You may find it helpful to offer a story problem suggestion to help them get started. End the session by asking each student to write a story problem for a subtraction expression that you provide and solve it.

❖ **Tip for the Linguistically Diverse Classroom** Suggest that students with a limited English proficiency use sketches and numbers to record their story problems.

Session 2 Follow-Up

 **Homework**

A Subtraction Story Problem Ask students to write and solve a story problem about a separating situation in which they begin with an amount, then remove part of that amount. Ask students to create a problem based on something they can see out of a window at home. Remind them to record their solution strategies using some combination of numbers, words, and/or pictures on Student Sheet 5.

The Relationship Between Addition and Subtraction

Problems with similar solution strategies may appear quite different to some students. We may assume that certain situations are addition and others are subtraction because we are used to thinking of them that way, but we may find that students solve problems in unexpected ways.

For this reason, as you introduce addition and subtraction problems to students, don't label them. A critical skill in solving problems is deciding what operation is needed. Further, many problems can be solved in a variety of ways, and students need to choose operations that make sense to them for each situation. For example, students may solve problems that you think of as subtraction by using addition (in fact, many adults solve problems of this type in this way). Consider the following problem:

Yesterday at the park, I counted 39 pigeons. When a big dog walked by, 17 of them flew away. How many were still there?

Most of us learned to interpret this situation as subtraction, and we may naturally assume that students should also see this problem as subtraction. Students who use counters to solve this problem will probably count out 39, remove 17, and count how many remain. However, there are many other ways to solve this problem:

- counting down from 39: 38, 37, 36, 35, . . . 24, 23, 22

- counting up from 17: 18, 19, 20, . . . 37, 38, 39; and keeping track of how many numbers are counted

- counting up by 10's: 27, 37, that's 20, and 2 more is 39; or, from 17 to 37 is 20 and 2 more is 39

- counting down by 10's: 29, 19, that's 20, and 2 more down to 17 is 22

- using landmarks, such as multiples of 10: from 17 to 20 is 3, from 20 to 30 is 10, from 30 to 39 is 9; 10 + 3 is 13 and 9 more is 22 (or 13 and 7 more is 20 and 2 more is 22)

- subtracting 10's and 1's: 30 – 10 is 20; 9 – 7 is 2; 20 + 2 is 22

Some of these methods are based on subtraction (moving from 39 down to 17), but others are based on addition (moving up from 17 to 39). Which method is chosen may have to do with a person's mental model of the situation: Do you see this problem as a "taking-away" situation to be solved by subtraction, as an adding-on situation, or as a gap between two numbers that might be solved by either addition or subtraction, depending on which is easier in the particular situation? The important point here is that all of these methods are appropriate for solving this problem. Addition is just as appropriate for solving this problem as subtraction and, for many students, makes more sense.

What Does It Mean to Be Finished?

In this discussion, which takes place during the activity on page 20, the teacher is trying to help students understand what it means to record their strategies so that someone else can understand clearly how they approached the problem. This is difficult for many students. Because their methods seem so clear to them, they think that what they wrote or drew explains their thinking even when there are gaps in their recordings. Taking the point of view of a reader of their work is a new skill for students at this age, and one that they will need to work on.

The teacher reviews with the class what the expectations are, then gives individual students feedback on the problem:

Today we're going to work on this problem: Yesterday at the park I counted 39 pigeons. When a big dog walked by, 17 of them flew away. How many were still there?

Before we begin, who can tell us what we should do as we solve this problem?

Samir: Sit down and try to figure it out.

OK, what else?

Paul: Write it down.

Who can say more about what you might write?

Olga: Don't just say like 62.

Jess: And you can't just say, "I used cubes."

Right, that's not enough. I wouldn't know what you did with the cubes.

Lila: But I just do it in my head.

OK, but you can write about what you did in your head so if I came and looked at your paper I would understand your strategy.

As the teacher observes Paul, she sees the following:

> Paul
> 39 - 17 = 22
> 39 ones - 17 ones is 22

I see the numbers in the problem and your answer, but I can't tell from this how you solved the problem.

Paul: I used cubes, but you said we shouldn't write that.

I'm interested in how you used the cubes. Can you show me?

Paul: I took 17 cubes, and I counted like this, 38, 37, 36, 35, 34, until I got down to the last cube and that was 22.

That's an interesting strategy. I don't think I've seen anyone else use that one today. What could you write so that someone could tell how you counted?

Paul added the following to his work:

> Paul
> 39 - 17 = 22
> 39 ones - 17 ones is 22
> I used 17 cubes.
> I counted.
> 39 ///////////////// 22

Continued on next page

continued

As the teacher observes Olga, she sees the following:

Olga

39 − 17 = 22
I used my head.

That's a good start, Olga. Can you explain more how you used your head?

Olga: I just knew it.

Well, sometimes that's true—the answer just kind of pops into your head. Suppose you wanted to tell someone else how to do this. What could you say?

Olga: Well, 39 minus 10 is 29, and then 29 minus 7 is 22.

OK, and what if that person said, "Where'd the 10 come from?" What would you say?

Olga: I broke the 17 into 10 and 7 because it's easier to minus a 10 first cause you know that 39 minus 10 would just be 29.

I've heard you use that strategy before. It seems to work really well for you to subtract the 10's first and then the 1's. When I was recording people's strategies, sometimes I used words, sometimes I used numbers, and sometimes both. How would you record what you just told me?

Olga: I'd use numbers.

OK, try doing that and then let me see if I can follow your thinking from what you write.

Only by continuing to insist that students record their work fully can you eventually help them imagine their audience.

Making Sense of Addition and Subtraction

Materials

- Counters
- Prepared envelopes containing Story Problems, Set C, cut apart
- Paste or glue sticks
- Student Sheet 6 (1 per student)
- Student Sheet 7 (1 per student, homework)

What Happens

Students solve a variety of story problems involving combining and separating, using their own strategies. Their job is to solve problems, check their solutions, and clearly record their approaches. Students are introduced to a new problem structure: combining with an unknown change. Their work focuses on:

- modeling problem situations
- selecting appropriate strategies for different problem structures
- recording strategies

Start-Up

Separating Problem Ask students about their experiences writing a separating problem for homework. You may choose to have students trade their problems with partners, then solve each other's problems. Or you can select several problems to read aloud to the whole class and ask students to solve them mentally. As you look through students' papers, observe their work to get a sense of whether they were able to create a separating situation that matched a subtraction expression.

Today's Number
- **Calendar Date** If you are using the calendar for Today's Number, brainstorm ways to express the number. Record students' expressions on chart paper.
- **Number of School Days** If you are using the number of school days as Today's Number, and the number is over 100, encourage students to break apart the number into parts, such as 100 + 12, and then offer suggestions for how to express one of those numbers, keeping the other intact. For example: 100 + 6 + 6 or 100 + 4 + 4 + 4. Add a card to the class counting strip and fill in another number on the blank 200 chart.

Story Problems

Students work on a variety of story problems representing different combining and separating situations. Show students the envelopes containing the story problems from Story Problems, Set C or the ones you have written. Explain that each story problem is stored in a separate envelope and that they can choose one or two problems at a time to work on. Students will need paper and glue sticks.

After you have chosen the problems you want to work on, paste them on paper. Use the space below each problem to show how you solve it.

Demonstrate for the class how to paste problems onto the paper. Depending on how much space an individual student needs, one or two problems can be pasted on one side of a page. Encourage students to work on one problem at a time so they can focus their attention on that problem and not feel as though they need to rush to finish many problems on one page.

The first page of the story problems contains combining problems (problems 1–6), and the second page contains separating problems (problems 7–12). These problems do not need to be done in any particular order. Students should not feel that they must get through all the problems, but monitor their work to be sure they solve both combining and separating problems.

As you circulate among students, modify the numbers in the problems as appropriate. Most students should start with the numbers given in the problems. However, after students have tried the problems with the given numbers, you may want to ask them to use lower or higher numbers. Students whom you are encouraging to do less counting by 1's may need lower numbers, while students who have developed flexible strategies of breaking numbers apart can try some higher numbers. *All* students should work with some combining problems in which the sum of the numbers in the ones place is more than 10 (e.g., 39 + 25 or 16 + 8) as well as some separating problems in which the number in the ones place of the initial quantity is less than the number in the ones place of the quantity being removed (e.g., 42 – 26 or 23 – 5).

If students have trouble understanding a problem, encourage them to visualize the situation and to describe or draw what is happening. See the **Teacher Notes,** Students' Addition and Subtraction Strategies (p. 32) and Developing Numerical Strategies (p. 33), for more about the approaches you are likely to see in your classroom. Discourage approaches that rely on individual words in the problem such as "how many left" or "altogether." Pulling individual words out of context distracts students from thinking about the structure of the whole problem. See the **Teacher Note,** "Key Words": A Misleading Strategy (p. 39), for more information on why this technique is not helpful.

Students work individually or in pairs. Remind them that they are to do three things:

- Solve the problem.
- Check the solution by using a different strategy.
- Record the solution so that someone else can understand it. After recording their solutions, they should check with at least one other student to see if someone else can understand their drawing and writing.

Over the two sessions, students should work on four to six problems. Two or three problems per session is enough if students are to solve, check, and record carefully.

Activity

Introducing a New Type of Addition Problem

During the last half of Session 4, gather students together. Explain that you are going to give them a different type of problem and that you'd like them to visualize and describe the situation. You should have read the **Teacher Note**, Types of Story Problems: Combining and Separating (p. 13), to familiarize yourself with addition with an *unknown change*. These are sometimes referred to as "missing addend" problems.

Close your eyes and see if you can imagine what's happening in this story. My friend has an aquarium with fish in it. She had 15 fish. Then she bought some more. Now she has 21 fish. How many fish did she buy?

Help students describe the situation without giving the answer to the problem. Ask questions such as:

What did the story look like at the beginning?
What do we know about what happened next?
What is it that you have to figure out in this problem?

You might draw a picture of the situation.

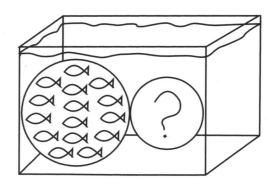

When you're satisfied that students can imagine the situation and understand what the question is, show them how to write this problem as a mathematical expression:

Sometimes we write these kinds of problems this way. [*Write 15 + __ = 21 on the board.*] **It means start with 15 and add some more to get a total of 21. We have to find how many fish were added. Who can think of a way we might solve this problem?**

Record students' suggestions. Then read problem 1 on Student Sheet 6, Story Problems, Set D, to the class. Tell them that this problem is like the fish problem—they have to find how much was added on. Give students Student Sheet 6. Ask them to draw a picture of the situation and record their strategies for solving the problem. Students can solve both problems on Student Sheet 6. Problem 2 is a subtraction problem with unknown change. If time permits, students can return to problems they did not complete on Student Sheets 4 and 5.

Sessions 3 and 4 Follow-Up

Discussing Addition and Subtraction   Students ask an adult when he or she uses addition and subtraction. They record the responses on Student Sheet 7.

 **Homework**

Students' Addition and Subtraction Strategies

As students develop strategies for problems about combining and separating, they are involved in two major tasks:

- understanding the structure of the problem
- developing numerical strategies for solving the problem

Understanding the Problem Structure   To understand the structure of the problem, students need to form a mental image or build a concrete model of what is happening. For example, if the problem situation involves putting together Anna's 14 marbles and Jose's 21 marbles, students need to be able to imagine the two separate groups of marbles and the larger combined group. They need to develop a mental model of the actions and relationships.

Combining is a natural activity for young students. Visualizing problems that involve separating or "taking away" can be more difficult. For example, suppose the problem states that there are 25 birds on a fence, and 11 flew away. The question is to find out how many birds are still on the fence. Some students begin to solve this problem by counting out or drawing *both* quantities, the 25 and the 11, then become unsure of what to do with them. In combining two quantities, the same action is performed on each quantity: Both quantities become part of a total accumulation. In removing or separating one quantity from another, however, one of the two quantities is a *part* of the other. The importance of visualizing the action is particularly critical as students model problems that involve taking one part out of a whole.

In order to visualize and describe the problem situation, some students will need to create a physical model of the actions. For example, students might solve the problem about birds flying away by drawing 25 birds (or tallies), crossing out 11 of them, and counting the number not crossed out. Or they may count out 25 cubes, remove 11 of them, and count the number remaining. These students are treating all the quantities in the problem as a collection of 1's

and are using counting as their primary strategy. Eventually, we want to move these students toward developing mental representations of the problem that allow them to work with larger chunks, for example, removing a 10 and a 1 or a 5, a 5, and a 1.

Students who feel more confident visualizing the problem mentally will be able to use strategies that involve counting on or counting back. For example, a student might solve the marbles problem as follows: "Jose had 21 marbles, so I counted 14 more: 22, 23, 24, 25, 26, . . . 34, 35." This student feels confident enough about visualizing the actions in the problem that she is able to hold the 21 in her head and add 14 to it, rather than counting out each quantity separately. Counting on—or counting back for subtraction—is a double-count situation. The student must simultaneously keep track of the numbers she is counting (22, 23, 24, . . . 35) and how many numbers she has counted (1, 2, 3, . . . 14). This double counting becomes even more complex when the student is counting backward. If a student counts back to solve the bird problem, he must count down from 25 (24, 23, 22, . . . 14) while at the same time counting up to keep track of how many numbers he has counted (1, 2, 3, . . . 11).

Developing Numerical Strategies   While students gain more experience in visualizing and modeling problem situations, they learn about the structure of numbers. As they learn more about number relationships, they begin to be able to take numbers apart into useful chunks, manipulate these chunks, and then put them back together. For example, they see that 25 is composed of a 20 and a 5, or two 10's and a 5, or a 20, a 3, and a 2. They use this increased flexibility in thinking about numbers to develop problem-solving strategies that don't depend on counting by 1's. See the **Teacher Note**, Developing Numerical Strategies (p. 33), for more specific descriptions of numerical strategies.

Developing Numerical Strategies

As students move from relying on counting by 1's to numerical strategies, researchers have found that students naturally develop strategies based on two ideas:

- Numbers can be taken apart into pieces that are more convenient to work with.

- It is often easier to work with larger parts of numbers first, then with the smaller parts.

Students in the primary grades typically begin to develop strategies for combining and separating problems like these:

Anna had 25 marbles and Jose had 11 marbles. How many marbles did they have together?

1. $20 + 10 = 30$
   $5 + 1 = 6$
   $30 + 6 = 36$

2. $25 + 10 = 35$
   $35 + 1 = 36$

3. $25 + 5 = 30$
   $30 + 6 = 36$

In the first example, the student breaks both numbers into 10's and 1's, adds the 10's first, then the 1's, then combines the two subtotals.

In the second example, the student starts with the larger number, adds 10 from the second number, then adds on the 1's from the second number.

In the third example, the student first breaks the 11 into 5 and 6 because she sees that she needs a 5 to get from 25 to 30. She adds on the 5 to the 25, then adds on the remaining 6.

There were 37 birds on the fence. 13 flew away. How many stayed on the fence?

1. $30 - 10 = 20$
   $7 - 3 = 4$
   $20 + 4 = 24$

2. $37 - 10 = 27$
   $27 - 3 = 24$

3. $37 - 7 = 30$
   $30 - 3 = 27$
   $27 - 3 = 24$

In the first example, the student subtracts the 10's from the 10's, then the 1's from the 1's, then adds the results.

In the second example, the student starts with the first number, subtracts the 10 of the second number, then subtracts the 1's of the second number.

In the third example, the student first breaks 13 into $7 + 3 + 3$ because he sees that it will be convenient to subtract 7 from 37 first. Then he subtracts each part of the 13, the 7, then the 3, then the other 3.

When adding, no matter how you break the numbers, you always add everything back together to get your final result. For subtraction, however, when parts are subtracted from parts, as in the first example above, the results are *added* together. Keeping track of what quantity you start with and what quantity is being subtracted, even when these numbers are broken into parts, is a critical part of understanding subtraction. Here is one student's strategy for $37 - 13$. This gives us some idea of the complex thinking involved in keeping track of the roles of each number in a subtraction situation.

> "Put the 7 from the 37 aside and save it. 30 minus 10 is 20. Then take away the 3 [*from the 13*] from the 20, so that's 17. Now add back the 7 you saved, and that makes 24."

Continued on next page

These are all strong, mathematically sound strategies based on students' good understanding of the numbers and their relationships. They are using knowledge about how a two-digit number is composed of 10's and 1's, about what happens when you add a 10 to or subtract a 10 from a two-digit number, and about combinations that make 10. These are the kinds of numerical strategies to encourage.

Students who learn to use strategies like these fluently and flexibly will eventually be able to solve any addition or subtraction problem. They will learn to modify these procedures to handle more difficult problems. For example, in the bird problem, if 19 instead of 13 birds flew away, the strategies must take into account that there are more 1's in the quantity being subtracted than in the original quantity. Students will not need to learn the historically taught algorithms that use carrying and borrowing because they will develop their own algorithms based on sound understanding of the structure of numbers and operations. For examples of student strategies for this kind of problem, see the Teacher Checkpoint (p. 37) in Sessions 5 and 6.

A Note on Notation   As students are learning to record, some may write solutions using a string of equals signs, like this: $25 + 5 = 30 + 6 = 36$.

This student is using the equals sign to indicate the sequence of operations being performed, but the equals sign is not used correctly here, since $25 + 5$ is not equivalent to $30 + 6$. Students may use symbols incorrectly as they work at developing their own strategies. When this occurs, model the correct usage for them.

Writing Stories for Numerical Problems

What Happens

Students write stories to fit numerical situations such as 28 + 15 or 33 – 18. They are introduced to both horizontal and vertical notation for recording addition and subtraction. They also continue to work on story problems. This is used as a Teacher Checkpoint opportunity. Their work focuses on:

- recognizing the meaning of horizontal and vertical notation for addition and subtraction
- matching situations to numerical expressions

Start-Up

Today's Number

- **Calendar Date** If you are using the calendar date for Today's Number, brainstorm with students ways of expressing the number. If students haven't included subtraction in their ways to express Today's Number, you might suggest that they try to do so. Record their expressions on chart paper.

- **Number of School Days** If you are using the number of school days and the number is over 100, encourage students to break the number into parts such as 100 + 15 and then offer suggestions for how to express one of those numbers, keeping the other intact. For example: 100 + 7 + 7 + 1 or 100 + 3 + 3 + 3 + 3 + 3. Add a card to the class counting strip and fill in another number on the blank 200 chart.

Materials

- Counters
- Prepared envelopes containing Story Problems, Set C remain available
- Paste or glue sticks
- Prepared envelopes containing Story Problems, Set E, cut apart
- Student Sheet 8 (2 per student, homework)
- Student Sheet 9 (1 per student, homework)

Introducing Notation

Introduce this activity by telling students the following:

You have created story problems for number sentences before. Today I would like you to create a story problem for this number sentence. [*Write 15 + 6 = 21, for example, on the chalkboard.*] Who can tell us a story for this problem?

Use numbers that all students can think about easily. Ask students to contribute a problem about this equation. For one or two of the stories, write brief phrases or draw a picture on the board to record it.

You may get examples of only the most familiar adding situation—joining two quantities. However, it's possible that students may suggest other problem structures that fit 15 + 6. For example, "I had 15 marbles. How many more do I need so that I would have 21?"

This problem and its solution can be recorded as 15 + 6 = 21, even though you might think of it as a subtraction problem. Students may not make the same distinctions we do about which numbers were given and which were to be found. Students will focus on their own perception of the structure of the problem. Since this situation can be modeled as either addition or subtraction, it is fine for students to record 15 + 6 = 21.

Show students both horizontal and vertical notation as a way to record these problems with numbers. If students have offered only one notation, ask them if they know any other way to show addition. If not, introduce both ways yourself:

$$15 + 6 = 21 \qquad \begin{array}{r} 15 \\ +6 \\ \hline 21 \end{array}$$

Next, write a subtraction equation such as 24 – 12 = 12 on the chalkboard and ask students to think about a story that they could tell for this number sentence. Record several stories and write the solution both vertically and horizontally. Throughout this unit, record problems both vertically and horizontally, so students become familiar with both notations. Make sure students know that they can still use their own strategies, even when a problem is written vertically.

Activity

Writing Your Own Story Problems

Ask students to write a short story for one combining situation and one separating situation and find the solution for each. Students can write the story in words or show it in pictures, then record the solution using numbers. Write problems such as the following on the board:

28 + 5   28 + 15   18 – 6   33 – 18

Students will need to organize their work on paper. Suggest that they fold a sheet of paper in half and do one problem on each half of the page.

After each story is completed, students can ask partners to solve it and to make sure the problem makes sense to a reader. As with their other work, encourage students to revise their problems in order to make them clear to others.

When all students are finished with their stories, have shared them with partners, and made necessary revisions, ask students to share their stories with the class. See the **Dialogue Box**, Stampeding Elephants and Other Stories (p. 39), for some story samples.

Students can share some of the stories they do for homework as well. For each story, record the problem and the solution. Sometimes use vertical notation, sometimes horizontal, so that students see both ways of recording.

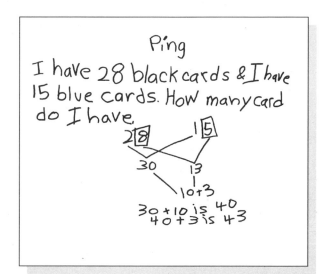

Laura
There were 28 pumpkins I wanted more so a person gave me 15 more. How many did I have all together?

$28 + 15 = 43$

29 30 31 32 33 34 35 36 37 38 39 40 41 42 43

Ping
I have 28 black cards & I have 15 blue cards. How many card do I have.

28   15
30   13
      10+3
30 + 10 is 40
40 + 3 is 43

Teacher checkpoints are places for you to stop and observe students and their work. This checkpoint is an opportunity to look carefully at the strategies students are using to solve problems.

During the rest of Sessions 5 and 6 students continue working on story problems. Add Story Problems, Set E (combining problems with an unknown change) to the collection of problems.

As you observe students, look at their papers to classify the strategies they are using. Look at one combining problem and one separating problem for each student. In particular, notice which students are counting by 1's to solve all problems, which students are building on number relationships they know, and which students are breaking up numbers in flexible ways. For example, you might review students' work on problem 11 on Story Problems, Set C:

In Kira's garden, there were 45 daisies. Rabbits ate 29 of them. How many daisies are left?

Following are three strategies you might see:

- Some students may count out 45 things, remove 29 of them, then count the number remaining.
- Some students may reason using important number relationships, for example: "From 29 to 30 is 1, then 10 more to 40, then 5 more to 45, so it's 10 plus 1 plus 5, that's 16," or "29 to 39 is 10 and then 6 more."
- Some students may use the base-ten structure of the numbers, for example: "40 take away 20 is 20, then take away 9 more is 11, and then put back the 5 from the 45, so it's 16."

If students are having trouble modeling subtraction situations, they may need more experience visualizing subtraction problems. For more information about ways students develop their approaches to addition and subtraction, see the **Teacher Notes**, Students' Addition and Subtraction Strategies (p. 32) and Developing Numerical Strategies (p. 33).

Sessions 5 and 6 Follow-Up

 **Homework**

Solving Story Problems   After Session 5, students who need more time can complete the story problems started during class. They can glue or staple one or two problems onto a copy of Student Sheet 8, Problem Strategies. Students who are finished can make up one or two more, using their own numbers on Student Sheet 9, Writing and Solving a Story Problem.

Solving More Story Problems   After Session 6, students can choose one of the story problems they have not completed to do for homework. They can glue or staple the problem onto a copy of Student Sheet 8, Problem Strategies.

"Key Words": A Misleading Strategy   Teacher Note

Some mathematics materials have advocated a "key words" technique to help students solve story problems. Students are taught to recognize words in a problem that provide clues about how to choose which operation to use to solve a problem. For example, *altogether* or *more* signal addition, whereas *left* or *fewer* signal subtraction:

I had 5 marbles. Sue gave me 6 more. How many do I have altogether?

I had 16 marbles. I gave away 8. How many do I have left?

I had 16 marbles. Sue has 7 fewer than I do. How many marbles does Sue have?

There are two flaws in the key word approach. First, these words may be used in many ways. They might be part of a problem that requires a different operation from the expected one:

There are 28 students in our class altogether. There are 13 boys. How many are girls?

If we trust in key words, then *altogether* in this problem should signal addition of the numbers in the problem: 28 + 13. The problem actually calls for finding the *difference* between 28 and 13.

The second reason for avoiding reliance on key words is that students should think through the entire structure of the problem. They need to read the problem and understand the situation so that they can construct a model of the problem for themselves. Here's another example:

I want to make cookies for my party. There will be 6 people at my party, including me. I want each person to have 4 cookies. How many cookies should I make altogether?

If students are encouraged to use key words, they are likely simply to pull numbers out of the problem and carry out some operation—in this case, perhaps, 6 + 4—without developing a model of the whole problem, a structure of 6 equal groups of 4.

D I A L O G U E B O X

Stampeding Elephants and Other Stories

Here are some of the stories that second graders wrote for 33 – 18 during the activity Writing Your Own Story Problems (p. 36).

Imani: 33 dolphins were jumping in the water, and 18 of them jumped to do a flip. How many of them didn't do a flip?

Phoebe: There were 33 little puppies in a pet shop. 18 broke out and ran away. How many didn't run away?

Ping: 33 robbers robbed a house. 18 of them got caught by the police. How many of them are still robbing?

Franco: There were 33 stuffed elephants in my bedroom. 18 came alive and stampeded in the night. The rest were peaceful. How many were peaceful?

Harris: 33 mice were eating cheese. They ate so much 18 of them died. How many were still alive?

We've found that death and subtraction and second graders are an almost inevitable combination. The following is one conversation overheard in a second-grade classroom.

Juanita: Beth had 33 cats and then all of a sudden 18 of them died. How many were still alive?

Oh, honey, you always have them die.

Juanita: Because I'm still thinking about my mice that died.

So you're still working it through.

Juanita: Yeah.

Students sometimes use story problems they create as a way to express their own fears and feelings. The teacher acknowledged Juanita's sadness without dwelling on it.

Working with 100

What Happens

Session 1: Exploring the 100 Chart Students are introduced to the 100 chart. They share observations about how the chart is organized and then use the 100 chart as a gameboard to play Get to 100, which involves adding multiples of 5 and 10 to total 100.

Session 2: Games on the 100 Chart Students are introduced to Choice Time. They continue playing Get to 100 and are introduced to a second game called Roll-a-Square, played on the 100 chart.

Sessions 3 and 4: Working with 100 Using the games Get to 100 and Roll-a-Square as examples, students discuss how to use the 100 chart as a tool for calculating the difference between any number and 100. Two new activities, Pinching Paper Clips and Story Problems About 100, are added to the Choice Time activities.

Sessions 5 and 6: Collect $1 Students play the game Collect $1, then continue working on Choice Time activities. Collect $1, along with Pinching Paper Clips and Story Problems About 100, are the Choice Time activities for these two sessions.

Session 7: How Many Paper Clips? Students solve a story problem about 100 in two different ways. They record each of their strategies in a way that communicates their thinking. The session ends with a whole-class discussion about the problem.

Mathematical Emphasis

- Becoming familiar with the structure and patterns of the number system from 1 to 100
- Using coins as a model for adding and subtracting multiples of 5 and 10
- Using the 100 chart as a tool for combining and comparing numbers
- Developing strategies for addition and subtraction
- Comparing numbers to 100

What to Plan Ahead of Time

Materials

- Overhead projector (Session 1, optional)
- Hundred Number Wall Chart with number cards and translucent pattern markers (Sessions 1–4)
- Number cubes labeled with multiples of 5: 2 per 2–3 students (Sessions 1–6)
- Game pieces and markers such as interlocking cubes, color tiles, buttons (Sessions 1–7)
- Counters (Sessions 1–7)
- Interlocking cubes: 1000 (Sessions 2–7)
- Number cubes labeled 1–6: 2 per 2–3 students (Sessions 2–4)
- Envelopes: about 8 (Sessions 3–4)
- Boxes of 100 paper clips: 10 boxes (Sessions 3–6)
- Paper plates or plastic trays: 1 per 2–3 students (Sessions 3–6, optional)
- Paste or glue sticks (Sessions 3–6)
- Plastic coin sets (real coins may be substituted), 30 pennies, 20 nickels, 20 dimes, 20 quarters: 1 or more sets per 3–4 students (Sessions 5–6)
- Paper money, $1 bills: at least 1 bill per student (Sessions 5–6)

Other Preparation

- Duplicate student sheets and teaching resources, located at the end of this unit, in the following quantities. If you have Student Activity Booklets, copy only the transparency and extra materials marked with an asterisk.

For Session 1

Student Sheet 10, Side-by-Side 100 Charts (p. 160): 1 per student (optional)

100 Chart (p. 190): 1 per student, plus 1 transparency*

For Session 2

Roll-a-Square Cards (p. 167): Duplicate on oaktag for durability. Cut apart to form decks. Prepare 1 deck per 2–3 students.

Student Sheet 10, Side-by-Side 100 Charts (p. 160): 1 per student (optional)

100 Chart (p. 190): 2 per student (homework). Students can use their 100 charts from Session 1 to play Get to 100 during math class.

Student Sheet 11, Multiples-of-5 Cards (p. 161): 1 per student (homework)

Student Sheet 12, Get to 100 (p. 162): 1 per student (homework)

For Sessions 3–4

Student Sheet 13, Pinching Paper Clips (p. 163): 1 per student, plus extras*

Student Sheet 14, Pinching Objects (p.164): 1 per student (homework)

Story Problems About 100 (p. 169) or copies of problems you have created: 1 per student. Cut apart into individual problems. Store the copies of each problem in a separate envelope. Paste an example of each problem on the front of the envelope so students can see which problem they are choosing.

Continued on next page

For Sessions 5–6

Student Sheet 8, Problem Strategies (p. 155): 1 per student (homework)

Student Sheet 13, Pinching Paper Clips (p. 163): 1 per student, plus extras*

For Session 7

Student Sheet 15, How Many Paper Clips? (p. 165): 1 per student

100 Chart* (p. 190): Keep available for students who want them.

Student Sheet 16, Writing and Solving Story Problems About 100 (p. 166): 1 per student (homework)

■ If you do not have the manufactured Hundred Number Wall Chart from the grade 2 *Investigations* kit, you can make one using heavy posterboard, paper fasteners, and white and colored index cards. Attach 100 paper fasteners evenly across the posterboard in 10 rows of 10. Cut 50 white index cards in half and punch a hole in the top of each one. Number the cards 1–100 and hang each card from a paper fastener. Cut the colored index cards in half and number from 1–100. These can be used to show a pattern in place of the transparent pattern markers. (Session 1)

■ Familiarize yourself with the rules of the games Get to 100 (Session 1) and Roll-a-Square (Session 2).

■ Prepare number cubes by attaching sticky dots labeled with multiples of 5. Use any combination of numbers on the cubes that are multiples of 5, for example: 5, 5, 5, 10, 10, 15. Prepare two cubes for each pair or small group of students. (Session 1)

■ If you have a blank 10-by-10 grid available with squares that match the size of interlocking cubes, duplicate this to be used as a gameboard for Roll-a-Square. (Session 2)

■ If you need additional multiples-of-5 number cubes for all students to play Collect $1, use Multiples-of-5 Cards from Student Sheet 12. (Sessions 5–6)

Exploring the 100 Chart

What Happens

Students are introduced to the 100 chart. They share observations about how the chart is organized and then use the 100 chart as a gameboard to play Get to 100, which involves adding multiples of 5 and 10 to total 100. Their work focuses on:

- becoming familiar with the structure and patterns on the 100 chart
- adding multiples of 5 and 10

Start-Up

Today's Number

- **Calendar Date**   If you are using the calendar for Today's Number, brainstorm ways of expressing the number. Suggest that students use combinations of 10 in their number sentences. For example, if the number they are working on is 23 and one number sentence is 10 +10 + 3, ask students if there is another way of making 10, such as (6 + 4) + (6 + 4) + 3 or (4 + 3 + 2 + 1) + (4 + 3 + 2 + 1) + 3. Record their expressions on chart paper.

- **Number of School Days**   If you are using the number of school days for Today's Number and the number is over 100, encourage students to focus on ways to make 100 using both addition and subtraction. For example, if the number is 118, solutions include 200 – 100 + 18 and 150 – 50 + 18. Add a card to the class counting strip and fill in another number on the blank 200 chart.

Materials

- Hundred Number Wall Chart with number cards and transparent pattern markers
- Multiples-of-5 number cubes (2 per 2–3 students)
- Game piece (1 per student)
- Student Sheet 10 (1 per student, optional)
- 100 chart (1 per student)
- Transparency of 100 chart (optional)
- Overhead projector (optional)

Before beginning the work in this investigation, it is important for students to have had experience constructing a 100 chart and looking for patterns. If you are doing the full-year grade 2 _Investigations_ curriculum, students will have had experiences with this in the unit _Coins, Coupons, and Combinations_. If students are not familiar with the 100 chart, add some 100-chart activities to Choice Time in Sessions 2–4 as suggested below.

Display the Hundred Number Wall Chart with numbers 1–100 in place.

What Do You Notice About the 100 Chart?

Look at the 100 chart carefully. Then turn to someone sitting near you and tell him or her one thing you notice about the 100 chart.

Ask one or two students to share their observations with the class. Students' comments may include descriptions, "The numbers go from 1 to 100." Or students may recognize patterns, "All the counting-by-10 numbers go down one side."

Record their observations in words on the chalkboard or on chart paper. Using the transparent pattern markers, highlight each observation on the chart.

1	2	3	4	5	6	7	8	9	10
11	12	13	14	15	16	17	18	19	20
21	22	23	24	25	26	27	28	29	30
31	32	33	34	35	36	37	38	39	40
41	42	43	44	45	46	47	48	49	50
51	52	53	54	55	56	57	58	59	60
61	62	63	64	65	66	67	68	69	70
71	72	73	74	75	76	77	78	79	80
81	82	83	84	85	86	87	88	89	90
91	92	93	94	95	96	97	98	99	100

All the counting-by-10 numbers go down.

1	2	3	4	5	6	7	8	9	10
11	12	13	14	15	16	17	18	19	20
21	22	23	24	25	26	27	28	29	30
31	32	33	34	35	36	37	38	39	40
41	42	43	44	45	46	47	48	49	50
51	52	53	54	55	56	57	58	59	60
61	62	63	64	65	66	67	68	69	70
71	72	73	74	75	76	77	78	79	80
81	82	83	84	85	86	87	88	89	90
91	92	93	94	95	96	97	98	99	100

All the numbers in the 50's are in this row.

Depending on students' experience with looking for patterns on the 100 chart, you may want to make available copies of Student Sheet 10, Side-by-Side 100 Charts, and have them color and write about a pattern they notice. You might also want to add this activity to Choice Time, if students need additional work recognizing number patterns.

It is important for students to become familiar with the structure and patterns on the 100 chart. See the **Teacher Note**, The 100 Chart: A Useful Tool (p. 48), for more information about using the 100 chart.

Get to 100

In Get to 100, students roll two number cubes (multiples of 5), add the two numbers, then move that many spaces on a 100 chart. The goal is to reach 100. After each roll, players record their move using addition, adding each subsequent roll on to the previous moves, as shown below.

Introduce the game by playing a few rounds with the class. Play on the overhead projector using a transparency of the 100 chart, or by gathering the class around a 100 chart. Begin by demonstrating how to set up the recording sheet.

Each player needs a recording sheet to keep track of the moves you make on the 100 chart. On paper, write your name, the date, Get to 100, and Game 1. For each game you play, you will keep track of your moves to make sure that they add up to 100.

Play a sample game to show students how to play and record their moves, using the Hundred Number Wall Chart. Place all number cards in the chart. Use the transparent pattern markers to record moves on the chart.

Explain that players take turns rolling the number cubes, moving along the 100 chart, and recording their moves. If on the first turn the roll is 5 and 15, the player moves a cube or game piece a total of 20 on the 100 chart and records these moves.

```
5 + 15
```

On the next turn, if the roll is 20 and 10, the player moves that amount on the board and records these moves.

```
5 + 15 + 20 + 10
```

At this point the marker should be on 50. As you play, invite students to help you add up the numbers rolled so far.

I rolled a 5 and a 15 and then a 20 and a 10. How could you add 5 + 15 + 20 + 10? Who has a way to start?

By listening to their strategies, you can get a sense of how comfortable students are with adding multiples of 5 and 10. Try to elicit more than one way of finding the sum.

Play a few more rounds until you reach 100. At the end of the game, players can choose to use only one number cube in order to land directly on 100.

After you reach 100, check your moves by adding the string of numbers you have recorded on your paper. It is not enough to write "= 100" at the end of your number sentence. I would like to know *how* you added the numbers and *how* you thought about the problem.

Demonstrate how to do this, using the recording of the game you just played as an example. Some students might suggest grouping certain numbers. Use arrows or circles to show this.

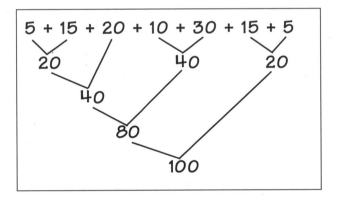

or

If your equation does not total 100, move your game piece back to where it should be and continue until you reach 100.

For the remainder of this session, students play the game in groups of two or three. Players who reach 100 can start over and begin a new equation. This allows the game to continue for all players.

Note: Students can save their gameboard in their math folders for use in the following sessions. Also, have students save their recording sheets. They will use these in Investigation 4, during the activity, Ways to Make 100 (p. 88).

Observing the Students

As students play, notice the following:

■ How do they move on the 100 chart? Do they move each amount separately, counting by 1's? Can they move in groups (a jump of 5, then a jump of 15)? Or do they find the sum of the numbers rolled, then move that amount?

■ How are students adding their number sentences? Are they confident as they add multiples of 5 and 10? You may want to make note of particular strategies for moving on the 100 chart and finding sums, then ask students to share their thinking during a discussion.

Five minutes before the end of the session, bring the class together to discuss the game. Some students might have questions about how to play. Ask some students to share their strategies for moving along the 100 chart and totaling the equations.

The 100 chart is used extensively throughout the *Investigations* curriculum as a concrete model of the number system and how it is organized. Because the 100 chart is a two-dimensional model, students can see all numbers between 1 and 100 and their relationship to one another. Students can see, for example, that 47 is composed of 4 rows of 10 plus 7 more; that it is 3 away from 50; that it is 10 more than 37 and 10 less than 57; and that it is almost halfway between 1 and 100. All of these are useful pieces of information when thinking about numbers and number relationships. In later grades, students use 100 charts to construct two-dimensional models of 1000 and 10,000. Once again they are able to think about the composition of numbers (1000 is 10 groups of 100) and where numbers are in relationship to one another.

When first introduced to the 100 chart, students are encouraged to make observations and identify patterns they see. Because the chart is organized in a 10-by-10 array, many important features of our number system are easily recognized. For young students, understanding the number 10 and its relationship to other numbers is an important step in developing sound number sense.

As students become familiar with the structure and organization of the chart and thus the structure of our number system, they can begin to use it as a tool for adding and subtracting. For example, consider the problem "How far is it from 29 to 53?" Some second graders will count on by 1's from 29 to 53, while others will efficiently use groups of 10. Some may use a combination of both strategies. What's important is that students understand the problem and recognize that they are finding the difference between the two numbers. The 100 chart offers students a model of the relationship between these numbers.

In this unit, students play number games such as Get to 100 and Capture 5 that utilize the 100 chart. These games provide opportunities for them to gain experience with the relationships of numbers on the chart. These experiences help students understand how our number system is structured. Understanding this structure supports the development of greater facility in adding and subtracting numbers.

Games on the 100 Chart

What Happens

Students are introduced to Choice Time. They continue playing Get to 100 and are introduced to a second game called Roll-a-Square, played on the 100 chart. Their work focuses on:

- using the 100 chart to keep track of a total amount
- adding multiples of 5 and 10
- accumulating 100 objects

Start-Up

Today's Number

- **Calendar Date** If you are using the calendar for Today's Number, suggest that students use combinations of 10 in their number sentences. For example, if the number they are working on is 23 and one number sentence is 10 + 10 + 3, ask students if there is another way of making 10, such as (6 + 4) + (6 + 4) + 3 or (4 + 3 + 2 + 1) + (4 + 3 + 2 + 1) + 3. Record their expressions on chart paper.

- **Number of School Days** If you are using the number of school days for Today's Number and the number is over 100, encourage students to focus on ways to make 100 using multiples of 5 and 10. This is similar to their work with the game Get to 100. If students are working with the number 120, for example, one solution could be 25 + 25 + 20 + 20 + 10 + 20. Add a card to the class counting strip and fill in another number on the blank 200 chart.

Materials

- Interlocking cubes (about 1000)
- Number cubes labeled 1–6 with numbers or dots (2 per 2–3 students)
- 10-by-10 grid with each square about 1" (1 per student, optional)
- Prepared decks of Roll-a-Square cards (1 deck per 2–3 students)
- Materials for Get to 100 (from Session 1)
- Student Sheet 10 (1 per student, optional)
- 100 chart (2 per student, homework)
- Student Sheet 11 (1 per student, homework)
- Student Sheet 12 (1 per student, homework)
- Hundred Number Wall Chart with number cards

Roll-a-Square

During the next few math classes, students will play two games that involve making 100. The first game, Get to 100, was introduced in the previous session. The second game, Roll-a-Square, was introduced in the unit *Coins, Coupons, and Combinations*. If students are familiar with this game, review it briefly. If not, introduce it by playing a few rounds with the class.

You will need number cubes labeled 1–6 and a 10-by-10 grid with squares that match the size of interlocking cubes for a gameboard (if available).

To play Roll-a-Square, you roll two number cubes, add the numbers, then snap together that many interlocking cubes to form a flat square. Each row of your square should have 10 cubes in it. Once a row has 10 cubes you can start a new row underneath.

After you roll and take your cubes, pick a Roll-a-Square card. Sometimes the card will ask a question and sometimes it will tell you to take more cubes or give some back.

Demonstrate how to roll the number cubes, collect the right number of interlocking cubes, and snap them together into rows of 10. Place the cubes on the gameboard if you are using one. After each turn, choose a card and read the direction aloud to the class.

My card says, "How many more cubes do you need to finish a row of 10?" I have 13 cubes now, one row of 10 and 3 cubes in the next row. How many more cubes do I need to finish this second row of 10?

Some students may automatically know that they need 7 more to get to 20, while others may benefit from counting the empty spaces from 13 to 20.

You might want to read a few more cards aloud so that students understand that choosing a card and answering the question are important parts of this game. Encourage students to listen to how their partner answers each question to make sure they agree with the answer. If they do not agree, suggest that they consult with another pair of students for help before they ask you.

When you have collected 100 cubes, your game is over. After you finish each game, unsnap your square and place the cubes back into the bucket so that other pairs of students can play.

Since each student needs 100 cubes in order to play this game, offer it along with Get to 100 and two activities on the 100 chart during Choice Time.

Introducing Choice Time

Explain to students that in math class they often will have the opportunity to make choices about which activities they work on. These sessions are called Choice Time.

If you are using the full-year *Investigations* curriculum, the Choice Time format will be familiar to you and your students. If this is your first experience with Choice Time, explain to students how they are to work during this time. See the **Teacher Note,** About Choice Time (p. 55), for information about how to set up Choice Time, including how students might use the Weekly Log to keep track of their work.

For the remainder of this session and for the next few math classes, students will play Roll-a-Square and Get to 100. Each student should play both games at least once, although students benefit greatly from playing games such as these over and over. See the **Teacher Note,** The Importance of Playing More than Once (p. 57).

If Roll-a-Square is a challenge to students, it will be important for them to continue playing this game throughout this investigation. Observing the Students (p. 52) can help you assess how they are doing with this game. At the beginning of Session 3, have a discussion about these games, highlighting how students are thinking about relationships among the numbers on the 100 chart.

Post the following list on the chalkboard. Included also are two optional activities on the 100 chart. If you have just introduced students to the 100 chart and to finding patterns on the 100 chart, you may want to include these activities as choices.

1. Get to 100

2. Roll-a-Square

3. 100 Chart (optional)

4. Patterns on the 100 Chart (optional)

Choice 1: Get to 100

Materials: Multiples-of-5 number cubes (2 per 2–3 students), game piece (1 per student), 100 chart (1 per student), paper for recording

Groups of two to three students take turns rolling number cubes and moving that amount on the 100 chart. After each roll, players record their moves (but not the total), adding on subsequent rolls to this equation. Play continues until each player reaches 100. Students check their moves by adding up the equation, which should total 100. Players can begin another equation when they reach 100.

Choice 2: Roll-a-Square

Materials: Interlocking cubes (100 per student), number cubes labeled 1–6 (2 per 2–3 students), deck of Roll-a-Square Cards (1 per 2–3 students), blank 10-by-10 grid (1 per student, optional)

Two or three players take turns rolling the number cubes and collecting that number of interlocking cubes. They snap the cubes together into rows of 10, until they form a 10-by-10 square. After each roll, a player takes a Roll-a-Square card and follows the direction. The game is over when each player completes a 10-by-10 square. (If you have 100 charts available on which interlocking cubes will fit in the individual squares, students can use these as gameboards.)

Choice 3: 100 Chart (optional)

Materials: Hundred Number Wall Chart and number cards 1–100

This is a choice for up to four students at a time. Students remove all the cards from the chart, mix them up, then reassemble the chart. Suggest that they deal the cards to each player and take turns putting the cards in the chart.

Choice 4 : Patterns on the 100 Chart (optional)

Materials: Student Sheet 10, Side-By-Side 100 Chart, colored pencils or light markers

Using the Side-by-Side 100 Chart, students highlight patterns they notice, then write a statement describing these patterns.

Observing the Students

As students work on Choice Time activities, you will have the opportunity to observe and listen to them. The **Teacher Note,** Keeping Track of Students' Work (p. 58), offers suggestions for recording and using observations of students.

The following are some specific suggestions for what you might observe as students work on Choice Time activities.

Get to 100

■ How do students move their markers along the 100 chart? Do they move each amount separately, counting by 1's? Can they move in groups (a jump of 5, then a jump of 15)? Or do students total the number cubes on both and then move that amount?

■ How do students add up their moves?

Roll-a-Square

- How do students add the total on the number cubes? Do they count on from one number or do they know the number combination?
- Are they able to answer questions on the cards?
- How do they calculate how far away they are from a multiple of 10?
- Ask students how many cubes they have collected. Are they able to use groups of 10 to find the total or do they count all from 1? Can they find how many more cubes they need to complete their 10-by-10 square?

Some students may still mostly be counting by 1's. It is important for these students to continue to play Roll-a-Square throughout this investigation or perhaps for homework. Get to 100 may be difficult for them. Compare your observations for both games. You may want to play this game with a small group of students so that you can gain a clearer sense of their strategies and difficulties.

100 Chart

- How do students place cards into the chart? Do they go in order or are they able to use the structure of the chart to place a card?
- Do they recognize and use patterns on the chart as they place the numbers?

Patterns on the 100 Chart

- What sorts of patterns do students notice and highlight? How do they describe in words the patterns they see?

Near the End of the Session Five or 10 minutes before the end of each Choice Time session, have students stop working, put away the materials they have been working with, and clean up their work area.

When cleanup is complete, students record on their Weekly Logs what they worked on during Choice Time. Suggest that they use the list of Choice Time activities that you posted as one reference for writing about what they did.

Whenever possible, either at the beginning or end of Choice Time, have students share the work they have been doing. This often sparks interest in an activity. You might ask two or three students to share what they did with the class, or ask a question that came up during Choice Time so that others can respond to it. Or you might ask students to explain how they solved a particular problem.

Session 2 Follow-Up

 **Homework**

Get to 100   At the end of Session 2, assign students to play Get to 100 with someone at home. Each student will need one copy of Student Sheet 11, Multiples-of-5 Cards, Student Sheet 12, Get to 100, and two copies of the 100 chart. Students can cut the multiples-of-5 cards apart at home. Remind students to record their moves in the form of a number sentence. They should write at least two number sentences for getting to 100.

About Choice Time

Choice Time is an opportunity for students to work on a variety of activities that focus on similar mathematical content. Choice Times are found in most units of the grade 2 *Investigations* curriculum. These generally alternate with whole-class activities in which students work individually or in pairs on one or two problems. Each format offers somewhat different classroom experiences. Both are important for students to be engaged in.

In Choice Time the activities are not sequential; as students move among them, they continually revisit some of the important concepts and ideas they are learning. Many Choice Time activities are designed with the intent that students will work on them more than once. By playing a game a second or third time or solving similar problems, students refine strategies, see a variety of approaches, and bring new knowledge to familiar experiences.

You may want to limit the number of students who work on a Choice Time activity at one time. Often when a new choice is introduced, many students want to do it first. Assure them that they will be able to try each choice. In many cases, the quantity of materials available limits the number of students that can do an activity at any one time. Even if this is not the case, set guidelines about the number of students who work on each choice. This gives students the opportunity to work in smaller groups and to make decisions about what they want and need to do. It also provides a chance to return and do some choices more than once.

Initially, you may need to help students plan what they do. Rather than organizing them into groups and moving the groups to a new activity periodically, support students in making decisions about the choices they do. Making choices, planning their time, and taking responsibility for their own learning are important aspects of a student's school experience. If some students

return to the same activity over and over again without trying others, suggest that these students make a different first choice and then choose the favorite activity as a second choice.

How to Set Up Choices

Some teachers prefer to have choices set up at centers or stations around the room. At each center, students will find the materials needed to complete the activity. Other teachers prefer to store materials in a central location and have students bring materials to their desks or tables. In either case, materials should be readily accessible to students, and students should be expected to take responsibility for cleaning up and returning materials to their appropriate storage locations. Giving students a "5 minutes until cleanup" warning before the end of an activity session allows them to finish what they are working on and prepare for the transition.

You may find that you need to experiment with different structures before finding a setup that works best for you and your students.

The Role of the Student

Establish clear guidelines when you introduce Choice Time activities. Discuss students' responsibilities:

- Try every activity at least once.
- Work with a partner or alone. (Some activities require that students work in pairs, while others can be done either alone or with partners.)
- Keep track, on paper, of the choices you have worked on.
- Keep all your work in your math folder.
- Ask questions of other students when you don't understand or feel stuck. (Some teachers establish the rule, "Ask two other students before me," requiring students to check with two peers before coming to the teacher for help.)

Continued on next page

Students can use their Weekly Logs to keep track of their work. As students finish a choice, they write it on their log and place any work they have done in their folder. Some teachers list the choices for sessions on a chart, the board, or the overhead projector to help students keep track of what they need to do.

In any classroom there will be a range of how much work students complete. Some choices include extensions and additional problems for students to do when they have completed their required work. Encourage students to return to choices they have done before, do another problem or two from the choice, or play a game again.

At the end of a Choice Time session, spend a few minutes discussing with students what went smoothly, what sorts of issues arose and how they were resolved, and what students enjoyed or found difficult. Encourage students to be involved in the process of finding solutions to problems that come up in the classroom. In doing so, they take some responsibility for their own behavior and become involved with establishing classroom policies. You may also want to make the choices available at other times during the day.

The Role of the Teacher

Choice Time provides you with the opportunity to observe and listen to students while they work. At times, you may want to meet with individual students, pairs, or small groups that need help or whom you haven't had a chance to observe before, or to do individual assessments. Recording your observations of students will help you keep track of how they are interacting with materials and solving problems. The **Teacher Note,** Keeping Track of Students' Work (p. 58), offers suggestions for recording and using your observations.

During the initial weeks of Choice Time, most of your time will probably be spent circulating around the classroom helping students get settled into activities and monitoring the overall classroom management. Once routines are familiar and well established, students will become more independent and responsible for their work during Choice Time. This will allow you to spend more concentrated periods of time observing the class as a whole or working with individuals and small groups.

The Importance of Playing More than Once

Games can engage students in important mathematical ideas. Most students enjoy the game format, so the potential for repeated experiences with a concept or skill is great. In addition, because most games are played with at least one other student, students are likely to learn strategies from each other. Whether playing cooperatively or competitively, students can learn a great deal from how others play a game.

While games have the potential to engage students in many important ways, it is only through repeated experiences playing the game that students can really begin to grasp some of the important ideas and skills presented. The first or second time a game is played, students are learning how to play the game. Once students have mastered the rules, they can begin to think about "What's the best move I can make?" and "How will my move affect my partner?" Many games do not involve a strategy but instead engage students in important mathematical ideas. In Get to 100, for example, an important transition for students is the shift from moving their game pieces by 1's along the chart to moving in jumps of 5 or 10. It is only through repeated experiences that students begin to understand that they will end up on the same number and that using groups is a more efficient way of counting.

Some games offer students repeated practice with skills such as addition combinations. In these games, students learn addition "facts" through frequent experience and familiarity rather than by rote memorization. Information that is learned through frequent use is less likely to be forgotten, and when it is, it can be reconstructed by relating the unknown fact to a known one.

Providing students with many opportunities to play games is critical if they are to benefit from them. Math time and Choice Time provide opportunities for students to play games. Offer these games to students at other times as well, perhaps in the early morning as students arrive, during indoor recess periods, or as choices when other work is finished. In addition, games are a wonderful way of communicating with families. One teacher made up game packs (directions and materials) in resealable plastic bags and used these as homework assignments throughout the year. Students often checked out game packs as voluntary "homework."

Throughout the *Investigations* curriculum there are numerous opportunities to observe students as they work. Teacher observations are an important part of ongoing assessment. Individual observations are snapshots of a student's experience with a single activity. When considered over time, a set of observations can provide an informative and detailed picture of a student. These observations can be useful in documenting and assessing a student's growth. They offer important sources of information when preparing for family conferences or writing student reports.

Your observations of students will vary throughout the year. At times you may be interested in particular strategies that students are developing to solve problems. Or you might want to observe how students use or do not use materials to help them solve problems. At other times you may be interested in noting the strategy that a student uses when playing a game during Choice Time. Class discussions also provide many opportunities to take note of students' ideas and thinking.

Keeping observation notes on a class of 28 students can become overwhelming and time-consuming. You will probably find it necessary to develop some sort of system to record and keep track of your observations of students. A few ideas and suggestions are offered here, but you will want to find a system that works for you.

A class list of names is a convenient way of jotting down observations of students. Because the space is somewhat limited, it is not possible to write lengthy notes. However, when kept over time these short observations provide important information.

Stick-on address labels can be kept on clipboards around the room. Notes can be taken on individual students and then these labels can be peeled off and stuck into a file that you set up for each student.

Alternatively, you might find that jotting down brief notes at the end of each week works well for you. Some teachers find that this is a useful way of reflecting on the class as a whole, on the curriculum, and on individual students. Planning for the next weeks' activities often develops from these weekly reflections.

In addition to your own notes on students, all students will keep a folder of work. This work and the daily entries on the Weekly Log can document a student's experience. Together they can help you keep track of the students in your classroom, assess their growth over time, and communicate this information to others. At the end of each unit, there is a list of things you might choose to keep in students' folders.

Working with 100

What Happens

Using the games Get to 100 and Roll-a-Square as examples, students discuss how to use the 100 chart as a tool for calculating the difference between any number and 100. Two new activities, Pinching Paper Clips and Story Problems About 100, are added to the Choice Time activities. Their work focuses on:

- sharing strategies for moving on the 100 chart
- calculating distance between two numbers on the 100 chart
- solving addition and subtraction problems involving 100

Start-Up

Playing Get to 100   Ask students to share their experiences playing Get to 100 at home. Have a few students share their equations for getting to 100 for one of the games they played.

Today's Number

- **Calendar Date**   If you are using the calendar date for Today's Number, brainstorm with students ways to express the number. Suggest that students use doubles in their number sentences. Record their expressions on chart paper.

- **Number of School Days**   If you are using the number of school days as Today's Number, and the number is over 100, encourage students to focus on ways to make 100 using multiples of 5 and 10. Add a card to the class counting strip and fill in another number on the blank 200 chart.

Materials

- Hundred Number Wall Chart with number cards and transparent pattern markers
- Boxes of 100 paper clips (10 boxes)
- Paper plates or plastic trays (optional)
- Materials for Get to 100 and Roll-a-Square (from Session 2)
- Student Sheet 13 (1 per student plus extras)
- Student Sheet 14 (1 per student, homework)
- Prepared envelopes containing Story Problems About 100, cut apart
- Paste or glue sticks
- Counters

Activity

Begin Session 3 with a brief discussion about moving on the 100 chart. You may want to display the Hundred Number Wall Chart.

In the games Get to 100 and Roll-a-Square, you had to find how far away from a number your game piece was, or you had to move a certain number of spaces on the 100 chart. For example, in Get to 100, if you rolled a 5 and 15 and your piece was on 20, how many spaces would you move and on what number would your game piece land?

Class Discussion: Moving on the 100 Chart

After students solve the problem, ask for volunteers to share their strategies. Some students may add the two numbers on the number cubes, then move the total number of spaces. Others may simply move their piece the designated number of spaces on each cube but not know how many spaces they moved in all.

Pose another problem about the 100 chart:

Suppose you were playing Roll-a-Square and you had 27 cubes arranged in two rows of 10 and a row of 7. After your turn you drew a card that asked, "How far from 50 cubes are you?" How could you find out?

An important idea to highlight in this discussion is moving by groups of 10 along the 100 chart. For example, to solve the problem above, students may say, "I thought 3 more to 30, then 10 more to 40 and 10 more to 50." Other students might count on by 10's from 27, saying "37, 47, then 3 more to 50." Encourage students to explain how they figured out the total number of moves from 27 to 50. To do this you might record both of these strategies on the chalkboard.

$$27 + 3 = 30 \qquad\qquad 27 + 10 = 37$$
$$30 + 10 = 40 \qquad\qquad 37 + 10 = 47$$
$$40 + 10 = 50 \qquad\qquad 47 + 3 = 50$$
$$3 + 10 + 10 = 23 \qquad\qquad 10 + 10 + 3 = 23$$

$$27 + 23 = 50$$

If time permits, pose another problem about distances on the 100 chart. The **Dialogue Box**, Moving on the 100 Chart (p. 65), is an example of how this discussion unfolded in one second-grade classroom.

Introducing Pinching Paper Clips

Introduce the activity, Pinching Paper Clips. Display the boxes of paper clips.

I have a new game to share with you. This game is called Pinching Paper Clips. Each of these boxes has 100 clips in it. In this activity you take a pinch of clips, count how many you pinched, and then figure out how many are left in the box. Record how many clips you pinched, how many are still in the box, and how you figured it out on Student Sheet 13, Pinching Paper Clips.

Discuss what a "pinch" is and demonstrate how to pinch some clips out of the box. In one class, students decided that a "pinch" involved using only the thumb and forefinger. Another group of students decided on the thumb, forefinger, and middle finger. Establishing a consistent "pinch" is not vital to this activity. Students may want to pinch paper clips in a variety of ways!

As students watch, pinch clips from a box, count the clips, and record the number on the chalkboard. Ask students to suggest ways to find how many clips are still in the box. Record strategies students suggest on the chalkboard, then explain to students that part of this activity involves recording a strategy for finding the number of clips left in the box.

Distribute Student Sheet 13, Pinching Paper Clips, to students so that they can see how they will record this information. Suggest that after they try this activity and record their strategy, students return all paper clips to the box and pinch again.

Students can keep Student Sheet 13 in their math folders until they are ready to work during Choice Time.

Choice Time

Post the following list of choices on the board:

> 1. Get to 100
>
> 2. Roll-a-Square
>
> 3. Pinching Paper Clips
>
> 4. Story Problems About 100

Explain to students that the following math session will be the last day for Get to 100 and Roll-a-Square. If they have not yet played those games, they should begin with one of them as a choice. For a review of the descriptions of Get to 100 and Roll-a-Square, see pages 51–52.

Choice 3: Pinching Paper Clips

Materials: Boxes of 100 paper clips; Student Sheet 13, Pinching Paper Clips; paper plates or plastic trays (optional)

Students pinch out some paper clips from the box of 100. They record how many clips were pinched and then figure out how many clips are left in the box. They show how they figured out how many are left in the box on the student sheet. Students will need to be careful to keep all 100 clips in their box. Providing a paper plate or plastic tray to work on helps students keep the clips in one place as they work.

Variation: Students take two pinches of paper clips and then determine the amount still left in the box.

Choice 4: Story Problems About 100

Materials: Prepared envelopes containing Story Problems About 100, cut apart (or copies of your own story problems); paste or glue sticks; counters

Students choose problems to solve and paste these problems onto paper. As students solve each of their problems, they explain their strategy using words and numbers. Explanations should be clear so that someone reading their papers would understand how they reached each solution. You may want to point out to students that Problems 7 and 8 each contain two questions for them to answer.

Observing the Students

Use the following questions to guide your observations as you observe students working. For a review of questions to help guide your observations for Choice Time activities 1 and 2, see pages 52–53.

Pinching Paper Clips

■ What strategies do students use to determine how many paper clips are left in the box? Do they count back from 100 by 1's or by groups? Are students able to record their strategies with numbers?

■ Do students use different strategies when they pinch a greater number of clips than when they pinch a smaller number? Are students able to record their strategies clearly?

Story Problems About 100

■ What strategies are students using to solve these problems? Are their strategies changing or evolving, compared to strategies they used in Investigation 1?

■ Do students use multiples of 10 in their solutions? Do they use the 100 chart as a tool?

■ Are students able to record their strategies in ways that are understandable to others?

Five or 10 minutes before the end of each session, remind students to record what they worked on in their Weekly Logs. Suggest that they use the list of Choice Time activities that you posted as one reference for writing down what they did.

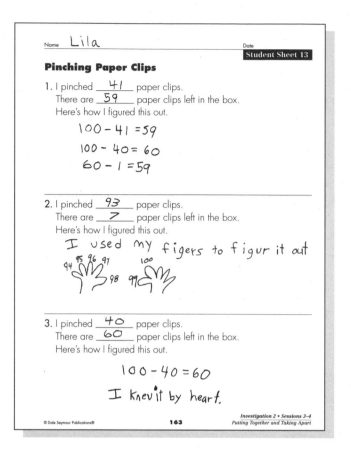

Name Lila   Date

Pinching Paper Clips

1. I pinched __41__ paper clips.
   There are __59__ paper clips left in the box.
   Here's how I figured this out.

   $100 - 41 = 59$
   $100 - 40 = 60$
   $60 - 1 = 59$

2. I pinched __93__ paper clips.
   There are __7__ paper clips left in the box.
   Here's how I figured this out.

   I used my figers to figur it out
   94 95 96 97   100
   98 99

3. I pinched __40__ paper clips.
   There are __60__ paper clips left in the box.
   Here's how I figured this out.

   $100 - 40 = 60$
   I knew it by heart.

© Dale Seymour Publications®   **163**   Investigation 2 • Sessions 3–4
                                                          Putting Together and Taking Apart

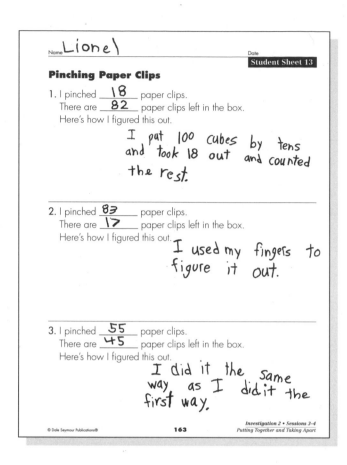

Name Lionel   Date

Student Sheet 13

Pinching Paper Clips

1. I pinched __18__ paper clips.
   There are __82__ paper clips left in the box.
   Here's how I figured this out.

   I put 100 cubes by tens and took 18 out and counted the rest.

2. I pinched __83__ paper clips.
   There are __17__ paper clips left in the box.
   Here's how I figured this out.

   I used my fingers to figure it out.

3. I pinched __55__ paper clips.
   There are __45__ paper clips left in the box.
   Here's how I figured this out.

   I did it the same way as I did it the first way.

© Dale Seymour Publications®   **163**   Investigation 2 • Sessions 3–4
                                                          Putting Together and Taking Apart

Sessions 3 and 4 Follow-Up

 **Homework**

Pinching Objects   Students play a version of Pinching Paper Clips at home. Instead of paper clips, suggest that they assemble 100 of some small object such as pennies, pebbles, or buttons in a plastic bowl. They can record their pinches on Student Sheet 14. Remind them to record their strategies for calculating their pinches. Suggest that students try the optional problem, and instead of taking one pinch, students take two pinches, then calculate how many objects are left in the bowl.

Note: You may want to prepare a few sets of 100 objects in small envelopes or resealable plastic bags in case some students in your class do not have access to such materials at home.

Moving on the 100 Chart

Thinking flexibly about numbers is an important idea in developing number sense. Just as we use familiar landmarks to find our way around, we also use familiar numbers such as multiples of 10 as landmarks in the number system. Tools such as the 100 chart can help students to visualize groups of 10 and distances between two numbers. This dialogue took place during the discussion Moving on the 100 Chart (p. 59).

Chen: I just counted up on the 100 chart from 27 to 50 and I got 23. [*Chen demonstrates his strategy using the class 100 chart. He counts confidently as he touches each number from 28 to 50.*]

Laura: I said 27 to 30 is 3. Then 30 to 40 is 10 and 40 to 50 is 10. Then I added 3 + 10 + 10 and got 23.

So Chen counted on by 1's and Laura went to a familiar number and then used 10's to get to 50.

Imani: I sort of did it like Laura, but once I got to 30 I just knew that it was 20 more to 50.

Naomi: I went back to 7 plus 3 because I knew that was 10, so 27 plus 3 would get you to the next ten. Then I added up by 10's.

So you used combinations of 10 to help you. When you first think about a smaller number, it can often help you think about a larger number. Any other ideas?

Phoebe: I counted up from 27 by 10's. I said 37, 47—that's 20—then 48, 49, 50 [*keeps track on her fingers*], that's 3, so it's 23.

Simon: I did it like Chen, but I came out with 24.

Can you show us what you did on the 100 chart?

Simon: I said 1, 2, 3, 4, 5, 6 . . . [*Simon begins counting on 27. He points to the 27 and says "one," thus including it in his total.*] . . . 20, 21, 22, 23, 24. [*He ends emphatically on 50.*]

Chen: Simon started counting on 27 and I started on 28.

Trini: I don't think you should count 27 because you're already at 27 and you want to know how much more it is to 50. So the first number you count should be 28. I think that's why you got 24 and Chen got 23.

So deciding which number to start counting on is an important decision. You also could think of the problem like this, "You have 23 marbles. How many more do you need to have 50 marbles?" Yes, Tory?

Tory: I have one more way. I went backwards to 20 because 20 to 50 is 30. Then I took away 7 from the 30 because it's really 27 and that was 23.

Naomi: I get it. It's like what I did except I went up to 30 and you went back to 20.

Collect $1

Materials

- Plastic coin sets (1 set per 3–4 students, add more coins if necessary)
- Paper money: $1 bills (at least 1 bill per student)
- Multiples-of-5 number cubes (2 per 3–4 students)
- Story Problems About 100 (from Sessions 3 and 4)
- Student Sheet 8 (1 per student, homework)
- Student Sheet 13 (1 per student, plus extras)

What Happens

Students play the game Collect $1, then continue working on Choice Time activities. Collect $1, along with Pinching Paper Clips and Story Problems About 100, are the Choice Time activities for these two sessions. Their work focuses on:

- using money to add multiples of 5 and 10
- calculating the difference between 100 and other numbers
- developing strategies for addition and subtraction

Start-Up

Pinching Objects Ask students to share the strategies they used for finding how many objects were left in the bowl as they did their homework for the previous session.

Today's Number

Ask students to express Today's Number using coin combinations. Suggest that students use combinations of 25¢, 10¢, 5¢, and 1¢ in their number sentences. If you are counting the number of school days, add a card to the class counting strip and fill in another number on the blank 200 chart.

Activity

Collect $1

If you are doing the complete grade 2 *Investigations* curriculum, your students will be familiar with the format of Collect $1. Versions of the games Collect 25¢ and Collect 50¢ are in the grade 2 unit *Coins, Coupons, and Combinations.*

To introduce the game Collect $1, you will need two multiples-of-5 number cubes, coins, and some dollar bills. To play, students roll the number cubes and collect that value of coins. Play continues, and on each successive turn, students trade coins until they can trade for a $1 bill. Students can trade in different ways. They are encouraged but not required to trade for coins with higher values as they play.

Demonstrate the game by playing a few rounds with a student. You may find that students vary in their approach to collecting coins. Some may take each amount on the number cubes separately, while others total the two numbers shown and take that amount in coins. After each turn, ask if a trade can be made for larger coins. After two turns, ask students to help you calculate your total value of coins thus far and how much more money you need to get to $1.

I have collected 85¢. How much more do I need to get to $1?

Encourage students to calculate their total amount after every turn, though most students do this eagerly without prompting! It is not necessary to play through an entire game—just play long enough so that students understand the game.

Playing in Small Groups   When students understand how to play the game, seat them in small groups and provide each group with the materials—number cubes, coins, and dollar bills. Groups should play at least one round. Remind students that part of the game is calculating how much more money they need to be able to trade for $1.

Choice Time

Post the following list of choices on the board. For a review of the descriptions of Pinching Paper Clips and Story Problems About 100, see page 62.

> 1. Pinching Paper Clips
>
> 2. Story Problems About 100
>
> 3. Collect $1

Choice 3: Collect $1

Materials: Multiples-of-5 number cubes (2 per 3–4 students), plastic coin sets (1 set per 3–4 students), paper money

Students roll the number cubes and collect that value in coins. After each turn, a player has the option to trade coins for other coins of equal value. Remind students to calculate how much more they need to reach $1 after each turn.

Variations: Students must have only dimes or only quarters in order to trade for $1 at the end of the game. As they play, they trade for dimes (or quarters) whenever possible, until they have enough to trade for $1. This encourages students to think about how many 10's or 25's there are in 100.

Collect $2 is introduced in Investigation 4 of this unit. Students should have repeated experience with Collect $1 prior to playing Collect $2.

Observing the Students

During these two sessions, try to spend time with each student. You may want to have a small group play a game with you or discuss their strategies for solving one of the story problems. Use the following questions to guide your observations as you watch students working. For a review of questions to help guide your observations for Choice Time activities 1 and 2, see page 63.

Collect $1

■ Do students take coins to match the amount on each number cube, or do they first total the two cubes, then take that amount in coins?

■ How do students collect their coins? Are they able to count out amounts by 5's and 10's (nickels and dimes), or do they count by 1's (pennies)?

■ Can students trade for a quarter in a variety of ways?

■ How do students make $1?

■ Are students able to determine how much more they need in order to make $1?

Sessions 5 and 6 Follow-Up

 **Homework**

Story Problems About 100   After Session 5, students choose one problem from Story Problems About 100, to solve for homework. They glue or staple the problem they choose to Student Sheet 8. Students should solve the problem and clearly record the strategy they used so that someone else can understand their thinking.

How Many Paper Clips?

What Happens

Students solve a story problem about 100 in two different ways. They record each of their strategies in a way that communicates their thinking. The session ends with a whole-class discussion about the problem. Their work focuses on:

- calculating the difference between 100 and other numbers
- recording problem-solving strategies
- using a different strategy to check a solution

Materials

- Student Sheet 15 (1 per student)
- Counters, cubes, 100 charts (optional)
- 100 chart (optional)
- Student Sheet 16 (1 per student, homework)

Start-Up

Today's Number

Calendar Date *and* Number of School Days Ask students to express Today's Number using coin combinations. Suggest that students use combinations of 25¢, 10¢, 5¢, and 1¢ in their number sentences. If you are counting the number of school days, add a card to the class counting strip and fill in another number on the blank 200 chart.

How Many Pockets? The routine How Many Pockets? gives students an opportunity to collect, represent, and interpret numerical data through an experience that is meaningful to them. As students collect data about pockets throughout the year, they create natural opportunities to compare quantities and to see that data can change over time.

How Many Pockets? is one of three classroom routines that occur regularly throughout the *Investigations* curriculum. The complete write-up of this routine, which includes several versions, can be found on page 138. If you are doing the full-year grade 2 *Investigations* curriculum, students will be familiar with this routine and you should proceed with the following activity. If this is your first *Investigations* unit, familiarize yourself with this routine and do the basic pocket activity with students *instead* of the following activity.

- **Calculating the Total Number of Pockets** Divide students into groups of four or five. Ask each group to find the total number of pockets they are wearing. Then collect the data from each group and record them on the board. Using this information, students work in pairs to determine the total number of pockets being worn by the class. Ask students to share the strategies they used to find the total.

Assessment

Solving a Problem About 100

Explain to students that you have been learning about their thinking by watching them solve problems and play games during Choice Time, and by reading their explanations about strategies they use to solve problems.

Today you will be solving a problem about 100 paper clips. After you have solved the problem, you will need to explain your strategy on your student sheet. Since I would like to get an idea about how each of you is thinking about this problem, you should work on this by yourself.

Distribute a copy of Student Sheet 15, How Many Paper Clips?, to each student. Review the problem together. Explain to students that after they have solved the problem and explained their thinking they should check their work using a different strategy. They can explain the strategies they used for checking at the bottom of the student sheet.

Materials such as counters, cubes, and 100 charts should be readily available for students who wish to use them. Remind students to include any tools they used in their explanation.

The numbers in this problem may be too difficult for some second graders. You may want to adjust the numbers for some of your students to make the problem accessible. In addition, some students may have only one strategy for solving this problem and therefore are unable to check their work using a different strategy. This is important information to note, and it can help you plan out next steps for your work with students.

If some students seem ready to work with higher numbers, make sure they solve the problem using a variety of strategies *before* you increase the size of the numbers. Developing and understanding a variety of problem-solving strategies allows students to become more flexible in their thinking and in their approach to solving problems.

Observing the Students

This activity provides an opportunity for you to assess students' problem-solving abilities. Observing students as they work can give you a sense of how they approach the problem. Their written work provides information about the strategies they are using and how clearly they are able to record their thinking. The following suggestions can be used to guide both your observations of students and your review of student work:

■ How do students approach the problem? Do they seem to understand the problem and readily begin to solve it, or are they more hesitant and unsure in their approach?

- Do students use materials to solve the problem? If so, which materials and how are they used? Are students mentally solving the problem without materials? For example, some students may model the problem directly using cubes or counters, counting out 63 and then adding on until they have 100. This strategy and use of tools differ from those of the student who uses a 100 chart to calculate the distance between 63 and 100 using jumps of 10's and 1's.

- Are students counting on from 63 to 100? If so, how? By 1's? By 1's and 10's?

- Are students counting back from 100?

- For students who worked with lower numbers, was the problem accessible to them? What sort of strategy did they use to solve the problem?

- Do students communicate their problem-solving strategies clearly? Does their written work explain their thinking?

- Do students have another strategy for checking their work?

- As you look through the set of papers, what do you notice about the class as a whole? Are most students using similar strategies for solving the paper clip problem? For example, do most students count on from 63 by 1's? Is there a group of students who are using 10's and 1's? By sorting the strategies into groups, you can get a sense of how your class as a whole is approaching this type of problem. If you find that students are using predominantly one strategy, say, counting by 1's, you may want to spend time looking at a different strategy as a way of expanding students' experience.

Plan a short discussion about the paper clip problem about 10 minutes before the end of the session. Encourage students to share the strategies they used. Then collect and review their papers. These papers can be returned and put in students' math folders. You may want to include this piece of work in the collection of work that students will assemble at the end of this unit.

Session 7 Follow-Up

Writing and Solving Story Problems About 100   Students use the collection of 100 small objects that they used at home for Pinching Objects (Sessions 3–4) to write and solve a story problem about 100. Students may use any format they choose on Student Sheet 16.

 **Homework**

Finding the Missing Part

What Happens

Session 1: Parts and Wholes Pairs of students play the game Cover-Up and record their strategies. Students share strategies in a class discussion.

Session 2: Problems with a Missing Part Students are introduced to a new problem structure—separating with an unknown change. Students solve and discuss a problem of this type.

Sessions 3, 4, and 5: Separating and Combining Choices Students work on three activities in which they continue to develop strategies for separating and combining problems. During Choice Time, they continue to play Cover-Up, work on a variety of story problems, and create story problems to match equations. The Choice Time activity, Solving Story Problems, is used as a Teacher Checkpoint.

Mathematical Emphasis

- Developing ways to approach different sorts of addition and subtraction situations
- Recognizing and solving problem structures with a variety of givens and unknowns
- Solving problems using numerical reasoning
- Recording solution strategies clearly
- Creating situations for equations
- Comparing solution strategies

What to Plan Ahead of Time

Materials

- Overhead projector (Session 1, optional)
- Counters such as buttons, color tiles or interlocking cubes: about 45 per pair (Sessions 1–5)
- Envelopes to hold problem card sets: about 18 (Sessions 3–5)
- Cloth pieces for covering counters (Sessions 1–5, optional)
- Paste or glue sticks (Sessions 3–5)

Other Preparation

- Duplicate student sheets and teaching resources, located at the end of this unit, in the following quantities. If you have Student Activity Booklets, copy only the extra materials marked with an asterisk.

    For Session 1

    Student sheet 17, Cover-Up Recording Sheet (p. 171): 1 per student

    For Session 2

    Student Sheet 17, Cover-Up Recording Sheet (p. 171): 1 per student (homework)

    Student Sheet 18, Story Problems, Set F (p. 172): 1 per student

    For Sessions 3–5

    100 Chart* (p. 190): Keep available for students as needed.

    Student Sheet 8, Problem Strategies (p. 155): 2 per student (homework)

    Student Sheet 17, Cover-Up Recording Sheet (p. 171): 1 per student, plus extras as needed for homework

    Story Problems, Set G (p. 173) or copies of problems you have created: 1 of each per student, plus extras. Cut apart into individual problems. Store each problem in a separate envelope marked with its number. Paste an example of each problem on the front of the envelope so students can see which problem they are choosing. See page 81 for the problem types included on those pages.

    Problem Cards (p. 175): 10 copies. Cut the sheets apart into individual problems. Put each problem in a separate envelope.

- Play Cover-Up to familiarize yourself with the game. Think about the strategies you use to play. (Session 1)

Parts and Wholes

Materials

- Counters (45 per pair)
- Cloth pieces or paper (1 per pair, optional)
- Overhead projector (optional)
- Student Sheet 17 (1 per student)

What Happens

Pairs of students play the game Cover-Up and record their strategies. Students share strategies in a class discussion. Their work focuses on:

- finding one missing part when the total and one part are known
- describing and comparing strategies

Start-Up

Today's Number

Calendar Date *and* Number of School Days   Ask students to use three numbers to express Today's Number. Suggest that they use both addition and subtraction in each number sentence. For example, if the number is 21 (calendar date), a possible combination is $15 + 10 - 4$. If Today's Number is 124 (number of school days), a possible combination is $100 + 30 - 6$. If you are counting the number of school days, add a card to the class counting strip and fill in another number on the blank 200 chart.

Activity

Introducing Cover-Up

To play Cover-Up, one player puts some cubes or counters on a table and counts them. Counts need to be accurate, so players should check their counts. One player then takes away some of the counters and hides them under a piece of cloth or paper. Together, both players use the remaining counters to figure out how many are hidden. Solutions are verified by counting the hidden counters.

Introduce this game by playing a few rounds with the class. So everyone can see, seat students in a circle and place the counters in the middle, or place the counters on the overhead projector. Put out 12–18 counters and ask students to count them. Secretly hide 3–6 counters and ask students to use the remaining counters to figure out how many are hidden. When the hidden number has been revealed, ask several students to share the strategies they used to find the amount.

Play several rounds with the whole class. Hide a different amount of counters in each round—a small portion, a large portion, and about half. This will give students the opportunity to use different strategies depending on the relationship between the total and the parts. With a total of 18 and 13 uncovered, students will often count up from 13 to find how many are hidden. With 2 uncovered, students may count down from 18. With 8 uncovered, some students may use the known fact, $8 + 10 = 18$.

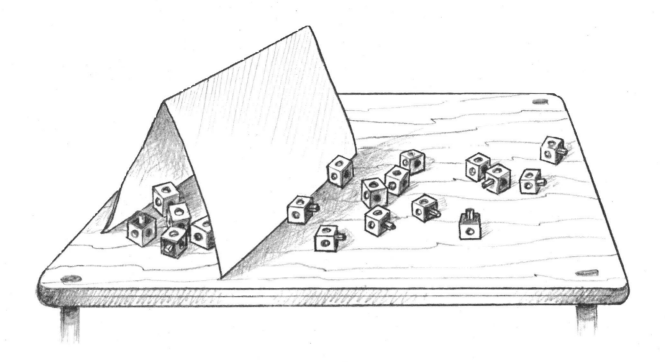

Show students how to record each round on Student Sheet 17, Cover-Up Recording Sheet. Then provide pairs of students with Student Sheet 17, counters, and paper or cloth to hide the counters.

Ask students to use 18 counters for a few rounds. As you circulate and watch students play, help pairs choose an appropriate total. Students should keep the numbers small while they are learning how to play this game. Imagining a missing part may be difficult for many students.

Class Discussion: Cover-Up Strategies

About 10 minutes before the end of the session, pose a problem for the class to solve and then discuss. Use the problem below or choose one that came up as they played.

I've got 21 pennies here. I'm going to cover some up. Help me count what's not covered: 1, 2, 3, 4, 5, 6, 7. OK, 21 pennies, 7 not covered. Who has a way to find out how many are covered?

Write on the chalkboard: 21 pennies, 7 not covered. Give students a minute to think about their strategies before sharing them with the class.

Record students' strategies in some way. See the **Dialogue Box**, Strategies for Cover-Up (p. 76), for the range of strategies you are likely to encounter. Counting up or back to solve problems can be difficult for students. Questions that come up may be similar to those that arose when students were counting on the 100 chart, "Which number do you start on? How far do you count?"

Strategies for Cover-Up

As these second-grade students discuss their strategies for the game Cover-Up, they see how others in the class approach this kind of missing-part problem.

Here's one from Graham's paper: They had 21 pennies, they covered some up, and they counted 7 that weren't covered. Think for a minute about how many they covered. [*Teacher writes "21 pennies, 7 not covered" on the chalkboard.*]

Lila: I got 14.

How did you get 14?

Lila: Well, I put 3 on the 7. That equals 10. Then I did 10 more. That equals 20. Plus 1.

So how did you get 14?

Lila: 3 and then 10, that's 13, and 1 more is 14.

The teacher writes:

$7 + 3 = 10$ $10 + 10 = 20$ $20 + 1 = 21$
$3 + 10 + 1 = 14$

Ping: I think it's 13.

You think it's 13? How did you get it?

Ping: I knew that 4 plus 3 equals 7. So first I did 21 minus 4. That's 17. Then I had to do 17 minus 3.

Where are you getting the 3?

Ping: I split the 7 into a 4 and a 3. So 17 minus 3 is 16, 15, 14. Oh, it's 14!

The teacher writes:

$21 - 4 = 17$ $17 - 3 = 14$

Temara: I went like this—8, 9, 10, 11, 12, 13, 14, 15, 16, 17 [*wiggles one finger for each number*], 18, 19, 20, 21. So it's 14.

How were you able to keep track of how many fingers you counted?

Temara: I was real careful. First I did 8, 9, 10, 11, 12, 13, 14, 15, 16, 17. That was 10 fingers, so I kept in my head that it was 10. Then I kept going, 18, 19, 20, 21, so 4 more. So it was 14.

The teacher quickly draws three hands with five fingers on each hand and writes the numbers above each finger.

Anyone have another way?

Jeffrey: It's kind of different. Mine's sort of like Temara's, except I made little marks while I counted and then I counted them.

Linda: I have a different way. I knew that three 7's is 21, so that means 7 goes into it three times. And 7 is one 7, and there's two 7's more. And I know 7 and 7 is 14.

Finding the missing part in Cover-Up is more difficult when the number of things not covered is relatively small compared to the number of things covered up, as in this problem. If 14 of the 21 pennies were showing, it would be easier to count up the number covered by 1's without losing track. Choosing a problem in which only 7 are showing encourages students to use numerical strategies rather than relying on counting by 1's. However, students who usually rely on counting by 1's will need to continue working on problems in which the covered number is relatively small. Encourage them to use grouping by 2's or to build from combinations they know. For example, if a student knows that 5 + 5 = 10, provide a Cover-Up problem with 11 counters of which 5 are visible.

Problems with a Missing Part

What Happens

Students are introduced to a new problem structure—separating with an unknown change. Students solve and discuss a problem of this type. Their work focuses on:

- finding the missing part in a separating situation
- recording strategies clearly

Start-Up

Today's Number

Calendar Date *and* **Number of School Days**   Ask students to write equations with a missing part to express Today's Number. If students are working with the number 25 (calendar date) they might suggest 20 + ___ = 25 or 50 – ___ = 25. If they are working with larger numbers, such as 125, a possible expression is 50 + ___ = 125. Record students' equations on chart paper and ask the rest of the class to solve them. If you are counting the number of school days, add a card to the class counting strip and fill in another number on the blank 200 chart.

Materials

- Materials to play Cover-Up (from Session 1)
- Student Sheet 17 (1 per student, homework)
- Student Sheet 18 (1 per student)

Activity

What Was Taken Away?

In this session, students are introduced to problems involving separating with an unknown change. This type of problem starts with a known amount, and some part is removed. The result is a known amount. Students find how much was removed (eaten, lost, spent, etc.). For a further description, see the **Teacher Note**, Types of Story Problems: Comparing (p. 109).

This kind of problem may at first be difficult for students to visualize. By playing Cover-Up, students began to think about how to find a missing part when the whole and one part are known. Start with a problem like this:

Teresa and Alberto were riding on a bus. They counted 25 people on the bus. At Market Street, some people got off. No one got on the bus. Then they counted 18 people on the bus. How many got off at Market Street?

Ask students to close their eyes and imagine the situation. What do Teresa and Alberto see at first? Then what happens? Ask students to describe what they know about the problem. Following students' descriptions, you might sketch "before" and "after" pictures of the bus.

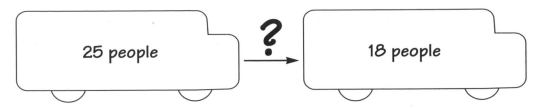

Ask students for some ways to solve the problem.

More "What Was Taken Away?" Problems

Read problem 1 on Student Sheet 18, Story Problems, Set F, to the class:

Mrs. Lee had 46 goldfish in her pet store. She sold some of the goldfish. Now she has 25 left. How many goldfish did Mrs. Lee sell?

Ask students to think about how this problem is similar to the bus problem. Some may recognize that both problems ask them to find how many were taken away. Distribute Student Sheet 18 to the class. Ask students to draw a picture of the situation and record their strategies for solving the problem. Encourage students to help each other make sure they understand the problem before they solve it.

Students who finish working on the first problem can try the second problem and/or play Cover-Up with a partner.

About 20 minutes before the end of class, gather students back together for a class discussion. Students can share their pictures of the problem as they tell the problem story in their own words. Then students share their problem-solving strategies. You may find a variety of strategies, including adding on and subtracting. Point this out and ask students to consider why this problem can be solved both by adding and subtracting.

Continue to find opportunities to ask students about the relationship between addition and subtraction as they work on similar problems.

Session 2 Follow-Up

 **Homework**

Cover-Up   Each student needs Student Sheet 17 to play Cover-Up at home with a family member. Talk about what students might use for counters at home (pennies, paper clips). Suggest that students use between 12 and 25 objects.

Separating and Combining Choices

What Happens

Students work on three activities in which they continue to develop strategies for separating and combining problems. During Choice Time, they continue to play Cover-Up, work on a variety of story problems, and create story problems to match equations. The Choice Time activity, Solving Story Problems, is used as a Teacher Checkpoint. Their work focuses on:

- finding the missing part in a separating situation
- recording strategies clearly
- visualizing what is given in a problem and what is missing
- choosing appropriate strategies for different problem structures

Start-Up

Today's Number

Calendar Date *and* Number of School Days   Ask students to write equations with a missing part to express Today's Number (see p. 77 for examples). Record students' equations on chart paper and ask the rest of the class to solve them. If you are counting the number of school days, add a card to the class counting strip and fill in another number on the blank 200 chart.

Materials

- Materials to play Cover-Up (including Student Sheet 17, 1 per student)
- Paste or glue sticks
- Prepared envelopes containing Story Problems, Set G, cut apart
- Prepared envelopes containing Problem Cards, cut apart
- Counting materials and 100 charts
- Student Sheet 17 (as needed, for homework)
- Student Sheet 8 (2 per student, homework)

Activity

Choice Time

Students work on three activities during these sessions—Cover-Up, Solving Story Problems, and Creating Story Problems. Solving Story Problems can be used as a Teacher Checkpoint.

Students are familiar with Cover-Up and Solving Story Problems. To introduce Creating Story Problems, write on the chalkboard 35 − 10 = ____ and 20 + 15 = ____ . Ask students to think about a story problem that would match each expression. Write one student's problem on the board and read it aloud. Talk about whether the story problem is clear and relates to the equation.

Then write an equation with a missing part, such as 20 + ____ = 30 or 30 − ____ = 20. Choose numbers that are easy for students so they can concentrate on the structure of the problem. Help clarify that an equation like 20 + ____ = 30 means "20 plus some more equals 30," or, "start with 20, add some more, and end with 30." See if students can create problems for this equation. The questions in their problems should be about the missing part. See the **Teacher Note**, Using the Equals Sign (p. 85), for more information about helping students connect equation notation with problem situations.

Post a list of Choice Time activities on the chalkboard. Students can work on one or two of these activities during each session.

---

1. Cover-Up

2. Solving Story Problems

3. Creating Story Problems

Choice 1: Cover-Up

Materials: 45 counters; Student Sheet 17, Cover-Up Recording Sheet; piece of cloth or paper

Pairs of students play Cover-Up. Help students adjust the total number of counters so they create situations that are challenging for them but not overwhelming. You may want to provide problems for certain students by writing them on their Cover-Up Recording Sheet. Students should record each round they play, but they do not need to record a strategy for each round. Instead, ask them to select one or two rounds and record their strategies on the back of the student sheet.

Choice 2: Solving Story Problems

Materials: Prepared envelopes containing Story Problems, Set G, cut apart; counting materials and 100 charts should be available; paste or glue sticks

Students work independently on a variety of story problems. Show students the envelopes containing the story problems (or alternate problems you have prepared). Explain that each problem is stored in a separate envelope and that they can choose one or two problems at a time to work on. Students paste the problems they select on paper, leaving enough space for them to solve the problem and record their strategies.

Make sure that students are recording their solutions and strategies clearly. If you don't understand what has been recorded, tell students which parts are difficult for you to follow. As they explain, students often realize how to clarify their recording. Ask them to revise their work so that it clearly reflects how they solved the problem. After two students have solved the same problem, ask them to explain their strategies to each other.

Students should be trying a variety of problems. The problem types included here are combining problems with unknown outcome and unknown change, and separating problems with unknown outcome and unknown change.

Addition, unknown outcome: 4, 5, and 10
   (depending on student's approach)

Addition, unknown change: 2, 7, and 9

Subtraction, unknown outcome: 3, 8, and 10

Subtraction, unknown change: 1 and 6

Note that problem 5 involves more than two addends, and problem 10 is a two-step problem. Students need to do a mixture of different kinds of problems so they get used to visualizing each problem situation and deciding how to solve it.

To make sure that students try each kind of problem, you can ask them to complete either all the even-numbered problems or all the odd-numbered problems.

Choice 3: Creating Story Problems

Materials: Prepared envelopes containing Problem Cards, cut apart; counting materials as needed

Students select a problem card and write their own story problems for the equation. You may need to help some students select cards with appropriate numbers. When students have written first drafts of their problems, they trade problems with a partner. Each solves the other's problem. Encourage students to give each other feedback on how to make the problem clearer. You may also want to read students' problems and ask clarifying questions. Students then do a final draft of their problem, possibly with a picture. Each student should write a problem for at least one addition equation and one subtraction equation during these sessions, including one equation with a missing part. These will be more difficult for students to write. See the **Teacher Note**, Using the Equals Sign (p. 85), for some information about notation and about ways to help students think about these problems.

❖ **Tip for the Linguistically Diverse Classroom** For students who are not writing comfortably in English, offer the alternative of using pictures to illustrate a story.

After students have written two problems, you may want them to select their own numbers and write one more problem. This enables you to see who is ready and eager to use higher numbers and whether students can use strategies they have been developing flexibly with larger numbers. Remind students that they must be able to solve the problems they create.

Make some of these problems into a book or duplicate some of them for homework or class work.

Observing the Students

These activities focus on addition and subtraction situations, including situations in which students are finding a missing part. As you observe students, use the following questions as a guide:

Cover-Up

- Are students counting the spots where they think the hidden counters are to "see" how many counters are covered up?
- Are they using numerical strategies? Are they flexible about choosing a numerical strategy depending on the situation?
- Do students count by 1's? Do they use some kind of grouping to count?

Solving Story Problems

Use this activity as a Teacher Checkpoint by observing students at work on the different types of problems. See page 83 for observation suggestions.

Creating Story Problems

- Can students create situations that match both addition and subtraction equations?
- Can they create problems for equations such as $46 + \underline{\quad} = 62$ or $55 - \underline{\quad} = 42$ in which the part added or subtracted is unknown?

As students work on Solving Story Problems during Sessions 3, 4, and 5, observe them as you circulate through the classroom and keep track of how students are interpreting each problem situation.

■ Which problem types are students able to visualize and interpret easily?

■ Are some students having difficulty understanding problems in which the amount that is added or subtracted is unknown?

Also look at the strategies students are using:

■ Are students counting by 1's? Can they count on or count back accurately, knowing where to begin and end?

■ Are students taking numbers apart in ways that help them solve the problem? Can they keep track of the parts of numbers they create and what to do with them?

■ Are students using 10's and 1's? Can they keep track of which parts to add and which to subtract? Can they easily combine 1's to make more 10's in addition situations? In subtraction situations in which they have to subtract a larger number of 1's from a smaller number of 1's, do they have good strategies for adding on or breaking the numbers into manageable parts?

■ Are students beginning to develop a repertoire of different strategies so that they can choose a strategy that works well for a particular problem?

Use a class list to note which problems students are doing successfully, which cause them difficulty, and what numerical strategies they are using. Use this information to determine what kind of problem you will use for the class discussion that follows.

If there is a particular problem that is difficult for several students, you may want to pull together a small group to help them visualize what is going on in that problem. Encourage students to think through the whole problem before they try to solve it. Discourage approaches such as relying on individual words in the problem that might seem to signal a particular operation. See the **Teacher Note**, "Key Words": A Misleading Strategy (p. 39).

Class Discussion: Story Problems

Choose one of the problem types that students are finding challenging for a class discussion during Session 5. You might choose a subtraction problem with unknown change, since that has been most recently introduced. Or choose a problem that has more than one step or has multiple addends. Devise a problem of your own with numbers that you think are moderately challenging for students. Pose the problem to the class and ask partners to talk about a strategy they would use to solve it.

Discuss the strategies as a class, listing them on the chalkboard. To focus students on classmates' explanations, ask another student to restate each strategy. For example, after Simon explains his strategy, you might ask:

Who can say in your own words how Simon did this problem?

Try this for one or two of the strategies students suggest.

Sessions 3, 4, and 5 Follow-Up

🏠 Homework

Find-the-Missing-Part Activities   Students can continue the Choice Time activities at home. You may want to assign one of these activities after Session 3 and a different one after Session 4.

- **Cover-Up**   Students will need a copy of Student Sheet 17, Cover-Up Recording Sheet.
- **Solving Story Problems**   Students choose a story problem to do at home and staple or glue it to Student Sheet 8, Problem Strategies.
- **Creating Story Problems**   Students choose a Problem Card and staple or glue it to Student Sheet 8, Problem Strategies. In the solution space, they write a story problem to match the equation.

Using the Equals Sign

Most of the equations students in the primary grades encounter have an expression on the left side of the equation and a single number on the right:

$6 + 10 = 16 \qquad 42 - 15 = 27$

They rarely see equations such as:

$20 = 40 - 20 \qquad 10 + 20 = 40 - 10 \qquad 9 = 9$

For this reason, students often believe that = in an equation means something like "now write the answer," rather than indicating equality between whatever appears on the left side and whatever appears on the right side. This may explain why, when students encounter an equation with a missing value such as $16 + \underline{\quad} = 20$, they often treat it as if it were written $16 + 20 = \underline{\quad}$. They see + and =, and these two symbols mean to them "add the numbers and write the answer in the blank."

When students encounter an equation such as $16 + \underline{\quad} = 20$, they may have difficulty interpreting it. Story problem situations can help students understand the notation.

I started out with 16 pennies. My aunt gave me some more. That's what the plus and blank mean here—add on some more, but we don't know how many more. Then I had 20. The 16 plus the extra together equal 20. So how many were added? We want to put a number in this blank so that the equation will be true. What number can you put there?

Try numbers students suggest. Then ask them to look at the completed equations and see if their number works. Use familiar number relationships in these equations to introduce this notation.

Working with the equation format is a good activity to do with students at different times of the day when you have a few minutes. Like Today's Number, this activity involves finding many ways to use numbers and operations to make equivalent expressions.

Here's an equation that has numbers on only one side. To make this equation true, we need to put something on the other side that's exactly equal to 6 + 3. Who can think of something that can go there?

Talking about the equals sign as a "balance point" may help students better understand equations—whatever is on one side of the equation has to *balance* whatever is on the other side. If one side equals 9, the other side also must equal 9.

$6 + 3 =$
Examples:
$6 + 3 = 9$ $6 + 3 = 7 + 2$
$6 + 3 = 10 - 1$ $6 + 3 = 3 + 3 + 3$
$6 + 3 = 59 - 50$

Adding Up to 100

What Happens

Session 1: Emma's Animals   Students share different ways to make 100. They are introduced to a story that involves the accumulation of 100 objects. In preparation for writing their own story, they write an equation that equals 100 using four to six addends. They exchange their equations with a partner and check each other's work.

Session 2: Ways to Make 100   As a class, students discuss examples of equations that equal 100. They then brainstorm possible contexts for 100 stories. Each student chooses a context, decides on an equation, and begins to write a story.

Sessions 3 and 4: Stories About 100   During these two sessions, students continue writing and illustrating stories about 100. At the end of Session 4, students share stories with partners. The Choice Time activities, Collect $1 (or $2) and Cover-Up, are available for students who finish early.

Mathematical Emphasis

- Working with 100 and combinations of numbers that equal 100
- Adding strings of numbers by "chunking" or grouping numbers that go together
- Writing a story that reflects an addition equation

What to Plan Ahead of Time

Materials

- Interlocking cubes or other counters (All Sessions)
- Students' recording sheets from Get to 100, saved from Investigation 2 (Session 1)
- Stuffed animals (Session 1, optional)
- Chart paper (Sessions 1 and 2)
- Paper, lined and plain, for story writing: 3–4 sheets per student, depending on length of the story (Sessions 2–4)
- Markers or crayons (Sessions 2–4)
- Number cubes labeled in multiples of 5: 2 per 2–3 students (Sessions 3–4)
- Plastic coin sets (real coins may be substituted): 1 or more sets per 3–4 students (Sessions 3–4)
- Paper bills: at least $1 per student (Sessions 3 and 4)
- Materials for Cover-Up from Investigation 3: 45 counters, Student Sheet 19, cloth or paper (Sessions 3 and 4)

Other Preparation

- Duplicate student sheets and teaching resources, located at the end of this unit, in the following quantities. If you have Student Activity Booklets, no copying is needed.

For Session 2

Student Sheet 19, Ways to Make 100 (p. 176): 1 per student (homework)

For Sessions 3–4

Student Sheet 17, Cover-Up Recording Sheet (p. 171): 1 per student

Student Sheet 20, Ways to Make $1 (p. 177): 1 per student (homework)

- Each student needs a recording sheet from one round of Get to 100, played during Investigation 2. (Session 1)
- Read "Emma's Animals" (pp. 90–91) prior to Session 1 to familiarize yourself with the story before reading it to the class. (Session 1)
- Bring in (or have students bring in) stuffed animals that can be displayed and used as props as you read the story "Emma's Animals." (Session 1)

Emma's Animals

Materials

- Chart paper
- Interlocking cubes
- Recording sheets for Get to 100 from Investigation 2 (1 per student)

What Happens

Students share different ways to make 100. They are introduced to a story that involves the accumulation of 100 objects. In preparation for writing their own story, they write an equation that equals 100 using four to six addends. They exchange their equations with a partner and check each other's work. Their work focuses on:

- combining numbers to make 100
- keeping track of amounts to be added
- writing equations with many addends

Start-Up

Today's Number

Calendar Date *and* Number of School Days Ask students to use multiples of 5 and 10 to express Today's Number. If the number is over 100, encourage students to focus on ways to make 100 using multiples of 5 and 10. For example, if the number is 130, one solution is 25 + 25 + 25 + 25 +10 + 10 + 10. If you are counting the number of school days, add a card to the class counting strip and fill in another number on the blank 200 chart.

Activity

Ways to Make 100

Students will need a recording sheet from one round of Get to 100 that they played during Investigation 2. Ask students for samples of equations that total 100 recorded on their sheets. Record their equations on chart paper.

Ask students what the addends in each equation have in common. Students may see they are all multiples of 5.

In Get to 100 you rolled number cubes and moved along a 100 chart. The number cubes you used had only the numbers 5, 10, 15, and 20 on them. Suppose that you could roll *any* number. What are some other equations for 100 that you might have rolled?

Give students time to think about this before you start accepting answers. As always, students' approaches to this task will vary. Some will come up with equations with many addends while others will look for familiar patterns such as 99 + 1, 98 + 2, and so on. You may want to stretch their thinking by suggesting the following:

Suppose I was making 100 using two numbers and the first number in my equation was 60. What number when added to 60 makes 100? [*Write 60 + ___ = 100 on chart paper.*] **What if my number was 66? Then what would I need to add to it to get to 100?**

Try a few of these with students. However, leave enough time for the next activity.

A Story About 100

"Emma's Animals," starting on page 90, is a story about students who collect 100 stuffed animals. Introduce the story by relating it to students' addition experiences.

Earlier in this unit we talked about ways of adding two numbers. Today we are going to talk about ways of adding more than two numbers. Here's a story about children who wanted to collect 100 stuffed animals for other children who lost many of their things.

Read the story aloud to students. As you read the story, write the number of animals each child collected on the chalkboard so that you end up with the expression: 5 + 10 + 10 + 23 + 2 + 20 + 4 + 1 + 20 + 4.

❖ **Tip for the Linguistically Diverse Classroom** If possible, gather together any stuffed animals you have access to, or ask students to take out any stuffed animals they brought into school. As a visual aid for students with limited English proficiency, class members can act out the story as you tell it. For example, ask someone to stand and hold up 5 stuffed animals to represent what Emma brings into school for the collection. If stuffed animals are not available, substitute a manipulative such as interlocking cubes.

Emma's Animals

One day in Emma's class, the children were talking about a flood in a nearby town. They asked Ms. Wright, their teacher, about the flood. "Many people have lost all of their things," Ms. Wright told the class. "Some of your friends and family members have gone there to help out."

Emma thought about this all the way home from school. She tried to think of ways she could help. That evening, she talked about the flood with her mother. "Do you think the children lost their toys?" asked Emma.

"Yes, I think that is possible," Emma's mother replied. "Many families are staying in centers until the flood is under control. They will not know what has happened to their things until they can return to their homes."

Emma had an idea. "Mom, I really don't need these 5 stuffed animals anymore. Do you think I could give these animals to the children there?"

"That is a wonderful idea," said her mother. "Perhaps some of your friends would like to give their stuffed animals also. Why don't you talk about it with them at school tomorrow?"

The next day, Emma could hardly wait to share her idea. She told the class about it during discussion time. "And I thought we could try collecting 100 animals," Emma told everyone.

"What a great idea," said Ms. Wright. The other children agreed. "But 100 is a pretty big number. How about if we collect the animals here at school? We can keep count to see how many we can collect. Then we can send all of them to the children."

There was quite a commotion in the classroom the following morning. There were animals everywhere. Emma had brought in her 5 animals. The twins, Ana and Carlotta, brought in 10

animals. Pete brought in his collection of 10 animals. "I've had these since I was four," said Pete. "I don't need them anymore. I would have had 11, but my little sister really wanted the yellow duck, so I gave it to her."

And Jamal and his dad brought in 23! "My dad works in a toy store," Jamal told everyone. "When he told his boss about our plan, he gave us all these animals for our collection."

Sari brought in 2 stuffed animals. One even played music. "I've had these for a long time," Sari said. "And, well, I'm tired of them. Hey, how many do we have?"

"OK," said Ms. Wright, "it's time for a math problem." Ms. Wright wrote 5 + 10 + 10 + 23 + 2 on the board. "How many do we have in all? Talk about it with someone sitting next to you. Then we'll solve it together on the board."

"Wow! 50 animals," said Pete. "We're halfway to 100!"

During the next week Aisha, Tory, and Paul talked to people in their neighborhood. They collected 20 animals. Ben, Jacob, and Jesse put their money together and bought 4 purple dinosaurs and 1 green elephant. "They're little," explained Jacob, "but I think someone might like them." Next came a huge bag from Charlie and Sui-Mei. "We got some of these from our rooms and some from our brothers, sisters, and cousins. There are 20 in all."

As Charlie and Sui-Mei were explaining their story, Mr. Sampson, the principal, walked into the room carrying a bag. "I heard about your collection," he said. "A few years ago the parents had a fund-raiser for the school and they sold stuffed bears. I found these 4 in my closet. They must have been left over."

Continued on next page

At this point there were so many stuffed animals in the meeting area there was barely enough room for the kids. "Do you think we have enough?" asked Ms. Wright. "I've been keeping track of the amount on the board."

$$5 + 10 + 10 + 23 + 2 + 20 + 4 + 1 + 20 + 4$$

"Now it's your job to figure this out. But before you start, who has a strategy to share about adding all these numbers?"

"I'd look for numbers that go together," offered Rishi. "I see some numbers that make 25."

"That's what I'm going to do," said Emma.

The students worked for a while. Excitement was building in the classroom. Did they reach their goal of 100 animals?

[At this point in the story, pause so that students can add this string of numbers. See the teaching suggestion on p. 92.]

As they shared their answers and their strategies for adding, most kids agreed that they had 99 animals. "We're 1 short!" groaned Pete. "I knew I shouldn't have given my sister that yellow duck."

Emma quietly got up, went to her cubby, and returned holding a stuffed red donkey. "This is Horace. I've had him for a while. He was special to me, but I think he will make someone else happy now."

The class was silent. Pete said, "Thanks, Emma. That's a nice thing to do."

Suddenly the class realized that with Emma's red donkey they had reached their goal of 100 animals. Everyone started to clap and cheer. "We did it! We did it!" Emma smiled.

"I think what you have done is wonderful," said Ms. Wright. You will make many children very happy. I am very proud of you." The children were proud of *themselves*.

Teaching Suggestion for "Emma's Animals" Write the equation on the chalkboard: 5 + 10 + 10 + 23 + 2 + 20 + 4 + 1 + 20 + 4.

When there are a lot of numbers in an addition problem, it's important to look at the whole problem. I notice that I can make a 25 by adding 23 + 2.

Circle or join 23 + 2 and write 25 to show that you have added these numbers. Ask students to suggest other addends that go together. If another group of 25 is found, students might also notice that they can add 25 + 25 to get 50. As students offer suggestions, circle the numbers and record the subtotal. Your recording might look something like this:

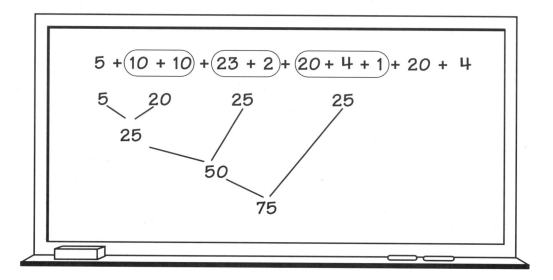

In this equation there were several groups of 25. In other equations you might look for numbers that are multiples of 5 or 10 and add them together first because these numbers are often easier to work with.

Read the rest of the story. Then add 1 to the end of the equation. Ask students to tell what the total is now.

If students have used the unit *Coins, Coupons, and Combinations*, remind them of their work with adding strings of single-digit numbers. In that unit, students looked for combinations of 10 or doubles. Looking at the whole problem and grouping or "chunking" numbers that go together is an important part of addition and subtraction. You may have noticed that some students approach addition or subtraction by counting all of the objects or counting on from one number, whereas others look for groups of numbers that can easily be added or decompose numbers into smaller parts that are easier to work with. See the **Teacher Note**, Moving from 1's to Groups (p. 94), for information about supporting students as they move from counting by 1's to counting by groups.

Equations for 100

The equation from "Emma's Animals" is one example of a group of numbers that can be added to equal 100. For the remainder of this session, students generate other equations for 100. Explain that each equation should have four to six addends (numbers) and should use only addition.

As you are thinking about which numbers to use, think about using numbers that go together just like in the equation for "Emma's Animals." So instead of choosing any six numbers, think about numbers that add to a multiple of 10 such as 33 + 17, or numbers that are multiples of 5 or 10, such as 15 + 20.

Generate a possible equation with the class.

Suppose I used 33 + 17 in my story. What does that equal, and how much more would I need to get to 100?

After students recognize that the sum is 50 and they need 50 more, continue with the following:

I need 50. I can't just add 50 because I have to use at least four addends. How can I break up 50 into two numbers that are easy to add?

Students may suggest 25 + 25 or 30 + 20 or even 39 + 11. If it seems appropriate, challenge them to think about how 50 could be broken up into three or four addends and record these equations on the board.

Students work on their equations for the remainder of the session. One hundred may be too large a number for some students to work with. Suggest that these students find equations that total another number, such as 30 or 50. A significant range exists in most classrooms. Just as you may have adapted numbers in story problems, you may make adaptations in games and other activities to meet students' needs. It is important for this activity to be accessible to all students and for them to be able to make sense of the numbers they work with. See the **Teacher Note**, Second Graders: A Wide Range of Students (p. 95), for more information about working with the range of students in your classroom.

At the end of this session, collect students' equations. Choose two or three that students can share during Session 2. You may want to choose equations that contain numbers that can be chunked or grouped.

Some students may solve addition or subtraction problems by counting all of the objects or by counting on from one of the numbers, while other students break numbers into parts or groups. Many students use a combination of these strategies. Here are some strategies students have used to solve 37 + ____ = 63:

- count all by 1's: count out 63, count out and remove a group of 37, count the leftovers
- count on by 1's: 38, 39, 40, 41, . . . 63
- count on by 1's and 10's: 38, 39, 40, 50, 60, 61, 62, 63 or 47, 57, 58, 59, . . . 63
- count by chunks: 3 more to 40, 20 more to 60, 3 more to 63; or 3 more to 40, 23 more to 63

All students should have opportunities to refine their strategies as their understanding of number and number relationships develops. Moving from counting by 1's to counting by groups or chunks and making use of 10's is what many students will be grappling with during second grade.

How can we help students refine their counting strategies in ways that are meaningful to them? Some students may be reluctant to let go of counting by 1's—even though they have the understanding to try other strategies. Through observations and conversations, begin to distinguish those who count by 1's because they cannot yet hold onto larger chunks of numbers from those who count by 1's because it is familiar.

Tim always solves problems by counting by 1's. The teacher has noticed that on work with the 100 chart, Tim can tell how far he is from the next multiple of 10 and wants him to make use of these bigger jumps when he works with addition and subtraction. He is working on 37 + ___ = 63.

How would you solve this problem?

Tim: I would count from 37 to 63 to figure it out.

How would you count?

Tim: 38, 39, 40, 41, 42, up to 63. And I'd keep track of how many by writing down the numbers.

So you'd start counting with 38. How far is it from 37 to 40?

Tim: 3. [*The teacher writes 37 to 40: 3.*]

And how far is it from 40 to 50?

Tim: 10. [*The teacher writes 40 to 50: 10.*]

Can you take another jump from 50?

Tim: From 50 to 60. That's another 10. [*The teacher writes 50 to 60: 10.*]

How much do we have so far?

Tim: 3 plus 10, that's 13. Plus 10, that's 14, 15, 16, 17, 18, 19, 20, 21, 22, 23. [*He counts on his fingers to keep track.*]

Now what?

Tim: 3 more to 63.

OK, so record that. [*Tim writes 60 to 63: 3.*]

Tim: 3 more, so that's 24, 25, 26.

Let's think about this. You just figured out how far it is from 37 to 63, but instead of counting by 1's, you used bigger jumps. Is there a way you can check that?

Tim uses his first strategy of counting by 1's to check his answer of 23. In this interaction, the teacher guided him through the process of counting by bigger groups and modeled a method of keeping track of the amounts. As Tim solved the problem, he used both counting by larger groups and counting on as part of his strategy. You will often see this combination of strategies, especially as students are moving from counting by 1's to counting by groups. When thinking about next steps for Tim, it would be important to observe how much of this new strategy he makes sense of and integrates on his own. Students do not always use the most efficient strategy that they are capable of using, but instead rely on strategies that they know best. Suggest that students solve the problem in two different ways, using one strategy to check the other.

Second Graders: A Wide Range of Students

In all classrooms there are students with varying strengths and experiences. With any activity you may need to make adjustments. In second grade there is a significant range of facility and understanding with the topic of number relationships and operations. Many students will be very concrete in their approach to working with numbers, feeling most comfortable counting by 1's, while others begin to make a transition to using groups and thinking more abstractly about a problem.

Adjusting numbers in story problems is one way to find the right level of challenge for individual students. This allows all students access to and experience with the type of problem being worked on. Students are more apt to focus on the structure of the problem and the strategy they are using to solve it if the numbers are familiar.

Consider the task in Investigation 4, Sessions 1 and 2, in which students write an equation with four to six addends that total 100. For second-grade students who are not yet comfortable with quantities over 50, this can be an inappropriate problem. They may be able to find an answer, but the answer may not be meaningful to them. Giving these students a lower number of 50 allows them to work with amounts that make sense to them, so that they can think about the number relationships and formulate a plan that is grounded in numbers they know.

Identifying each student's comfort level comes through observation, discussion, and looking at student work. Sometimes students' abilities to verbalize solutions or successfully play a game can mask gaps in understanding. Only by probing their thinking with questions can you discover how students are thinking. It is tempting to think that students know something because of previous experience or because of their age or grade. In reality, we know that the only successful way of moving students ahead is by offering them problems, activities, and questions that challenge them.

Ways to Make 100

Materials

- Students' equations for 100 from Session 1
- Paper, lined or blank, for story writing (enough for the class)
- Markers or crayons
- Counters
- Student Sheet 19 (1 per student, homework)

What Happens

As a class, students discuss examples of equations that equal 100. They then brainstorm possible contexts for stories about 100. Each student chooses a context, decides on an equation, and begins to write a story. Their work focuses on:

- writing an equation with many addends that totals 100
- writing a story to go with an equation
- "chunking" or grouping numbers to simplify an equation

Start-Up

Today's Number

Calendar Date *and* Number of School Days Ask students to use multiples of 5 and 10 to express Today's Number (see p. 88 for examples). If you are counting the number of school days, add a card to the class counting strip and fill in another number on the blank 200 chart.

Activity

Class Discussion: Equations for 100

Discuss two or three equations for 100 that students generated during the previous session. Choose equations that contain numbers that can be chunked or grouped in order to simplify the equation. One at a time students can write their equations on the board, overhead, or chart paper for the class to solve.

The following is an equation from one second grader:

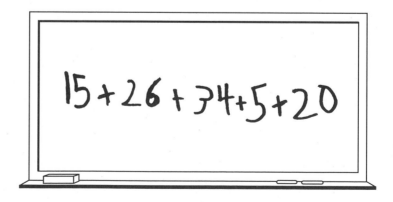

Look at Jeffrey's equation. Think carefully about the numbers. Do you see any that make sense to put together?

Students may suggest grouping 15 and 5 to make 20, then adding 20 and 20 to make 40. To add 26 and 34 students might add 30 and 20 to make 50, then add 6 and 4 to make 10. They then add 40 + 50 + 10.

Other students may suggest breaking apart the numbers to simplify them. For example, one student suggested: "Take 1 off of 26 and add it to the 34 to make 35. Then all the numbers are multiples of 5 and that's easier to add." She ended up adding the equation: 15 + 25 + 35 + 5 + 20.

Discuss a few more examples. If students are having difficulty seeing combinations of numbers, remind them to look for combinations of 10 or numbers that end in 5 or 0 (multiples of 5 and 10). The **Dialogue Box**, Ways to Make 100 (p. 98), is an example of how one teacher integrated Today's Number into this activity.

Choosing a Story and an Equation

During the next few days you will be writing math stories about the number 100. Your story should be different from "Emma's Animals," since you can choose different characters and a different theme. But your story should be the same as "Emma's Animals" in one important way: It should be a story about collecting groups of things, with the goal being to collect 100.

Brainstorm with students some possible scenarios for their stories. Here are a few ideas that could be considered:

- A boy who collects bottle caps, rocks, or shells.
- A group of three friends who collect bottles or cans for recycling. In order to redeem the cans, they have to collect them in bags of 100.
- A family has a party and invites some friends. Each friend brings a group of other friends to the party.
- A girl collects pennies from her family. Each person gives her the pennies in his or her pockets. Her granddad gives her all of his change.

When you have an idea for your story, think about the numbers you are going to use. You may want to use an equation that you created during the last math session, or make up a new one. Use four or five numbers and choose numbers that go together. When you have finished your 100 story, trade papers with a partner and solve each other's story problems.

Students will have time to write their stories during the next two math sessions. If you have a designated writing time during the day, students can work on their stories at that time as well.

Distribute paper. Encourage students to brainstorm ideas together, but each student should write his or her own story. You may want students to show you their equations and story ideas before they begin writing.

At the end of Session 4, students will share their stories with classmates.

Session 2 Follow-Up

 **Homework**   **Ways to Make 100**   Students generate ways to make 100 using any operation. They record their work on Student Sheet 19.

— D I A L O G U E   B O X —

Ways to Make 100

During this discussion, the teacher has integrated writing equations for 100 with Today's Number.

Think about Today's Number, 132, as 100 + 32. [*Teacher writes 100 + 32 on the chalkboard.*] **I'd like you to keep the 32 as a whole group but break apart the 100. Think about your work with the game Get to 100 and with writing equations that equal 100. In both activities, you were figuring out ways to make 100. Who has a way to break up the 100 part of 132?**

Temara: 50 + 50 + 32.

Ping: 70 + 30 + 32.

Laura: 60 + 40 + 32. Think of combinations for making 10 and add a zero for ways to make 100.

What do you mean, add a zero?

Laura: Well, 6 and 4 is 10, right? So just add zeros onto the 6 and 4. 60 and 40 is 100.

The teacher asks the class to list all the ways to make 100 using multiples of 10: 10 + 90, 20 + 80, and so on.

Tim: I found a long one. 15 + 25 + 10 + 25 + 5 + 10 + 10. Wait—let me just count this. 15 and 25 is 40, 25 and 5 is 30, and three 10's is 30. OK, so 40 and 30, 70 and 30—that's 100 plus 32.

That is a long one. I noticed that when Tim was adding up the numbers he looked for groups that went together, like the three 10's and the 25 and 5. OK, another one?

Imani: This is sort of like Tim's. 10 + 10 + 10 + 5 + 5 + 10 + 5 + 5 + 10 + 5 + 5 + 10 + 32.

Do you want to check that?

Imani: Let's see, 10, 20, 30, 40, 50, 60, that's the 10's. Then 10, 20, 30, that the 5's. [*She circles the groups of 5 as she counts.*] Whoops, I need 10 more!

OK, any other ideas?

Lionel: 10 plus 10.

Is how much?

Lionel: 20. Plus 30 plus 40.

And that gets you to?

Lionel: [*says quietly, 20, 30, 40, 50, 60, 70, 80, 90*] 90! Plus 10, plus 32!

Good thinking. I noticed that today everyone made expressions using only addition. For tomorrow's number, I'd like you to think about using just subtraction or both addition and subtraction when you suggest ways for making 100.

Stories About 100

What Happens

During these two sessions, students continue writing and illustrating stories about 100. At the end of Session 4, students share stories with partners. The Choice Time activities, Collect $1 (or $2) and Cover-Up, are available for students who finish early. Their work focuses on:

- writing a story to go with an equation
- solving stories about 100

Start-Up

Ways to Make 100   Have students post the expressions for 100 that they found for homework on chart paper. Small groups can meet together to compare their lists, noting any duplicates. Groups can take turns listing their expressions. Students can add to the lists over time.

Today's Number

Calendar Date *and* Number of Days in School   Ask students to generate expressions for Today's Number using four to six addends. Encourage them to choose numbers that go together (are easily added or subtracted), similar to the equations they made for their stories about 100. For example, if Today's Number is 132, an expression is: $25 + 50 + 25 + 20 + 10 + 2$. If you are counting the number of school days, add a card to the class counting strip and fill in another number on the blank 200 chart.

How Many Pockets?   Sometime during the next two days, collect data about the number of pockets being worn by the students in the class. Students compare these data to the pocket data they collected in Investigation 2 and figure out the difference.

Materials

- Students' stories about 100 from Session 2
- Markers or crayons
- Materials for Cover-Up
- Plastic coin sets (1 set per 3–4 students; add more coins if necessary)
- Paper bills (at least $1 per student)
- Multiples-of-5 number cubes (2 per 2–3 students)
- Student Sheet 17 (1 per student)
- Student Sheet 20 (1 per student, homework)

Activity

For Session 3 and part of Session 4, students continue to write and illustrate their stories about 100. During this time you may want to meet with individuals or small groups about their stories. As students finish, offer feedback or suggestions for refinement. Some teachers who use the process approach to writing have had students do a final draft of their story, with illustrations. You will need to decide how much editing and refinement to expect of your students based on their prior writing experiences.

Writing Stories About 100

Examples of students' stories in the **Teacher Note**, Stories About 100 (p. 102), demonstrate the range of ideas and kinds of numbers that students are comfortable working with.

Activity

Choice Time

For students who finish their stories early or need to take a break from writing during these two sessions, the activities of Cover-Up and Collect $2 should be available. Post the following list of activities on the chalkboard:

> 1. Cover-Up
>
> 2. Collect $2

For a review of the description for Choice 1, see page 74, and for Choice 2, see page 67. Collect $2 is a variation of the game Collect $1.

Introduce Collect $2 to pairs of students as they are ready to play. The rules are the same as Collect $1 except that the goal is to collect $2. Students will need coins and two multiples-of-5 number cubes. Remind them that after each turn, they calculate how much more money they need to reach $2.

Activity

Sharing Stories About 100

Plan about 20 minutes at the end of Session 4 for students to share their stories. During this initial sharing session, organize students into pairs. Each student should have his or her story about 100 and paper and pencil for recording.

Share your story with a partner. Each of you will take turns reading your story. As you are listening to your partner's story, write down the numbers in the story that are being added. When you have both read your stories, solve the problems in the stories. Then write your name and your partner's name on your recording sheet.

As pairs of students are sharing, circulate around the room and observe how students are recording the information from the story they are listening to. You may need to remind students to write the numbers in the form of an addition expression rather than just writing the numbers all over their paper.

As you solve your partner's story problem, remember to look for numbers that can be grouped together. Also, you will be checking your partner's work to make sure the numbers add up to 100. If they don't add to 100, you and your partner should go back and first check the numbers from the story, then check how the numbers were added.

If there is time at the end of this session or at some other time during the day, you may want to have students share examples of the equations from their 100 stories.

Sessions 3 and 4 Follow-Up

Ways to Make $1   After Session 3, students generate as many ways to make $1 as they can find, using nickels, dimes, and quarters. They list them on Student Sheet 20.

 **Homework**

Sharing Stories in Other Ways   Consider sharing students' stories as follows:

 **Extension**

- Bind the stories together in a class book. Read and solve one story each day. When the class has solved all of the stories, the book can circulate to students' homes to share with families.
- Join with another second- or third-grade classroom and have students share their stories.
- Create a bulletin board of stories about 100. Include the equation that goes along with each story and suggest that observers try to solve each equation.

This activity offers students the opportunity to integrate mathematics and writing. Because the goal is to write a story, students must first consider which numbers will be appropriate to use. One aspect of this activity is having students think about numbers that can easily be combined because they have some relationship to each other; for example, multiples of 10 or combinations of 10.

In any second-grade class there will be a variety of writing abilities and kinds of numbers with which students are comfortable. The stories below represent both and are offered as examples of what you might expect in your classroom.

Laura

One day I got $10 and my sister got $20 for her birthay. And then my brother got $30. My father got $40 for me. Now we have 100.

$$10 + 20 = 30$$
$$+ 30$$
$$\overline{60}$$
$$+ 40$$
$$\overline{100}$$

Laura's story is clear and direct. She uses four addends that are all multiples of 10.

Lionel

I had 14 rocks, then I got 39 more. When Dad went on a long bisness trip he got 1 For me. Then I bought 26. I got 14 for my birthday. My sister give me 6 more.

⟨4⟩ Save box

$$10 + 39 + 1 = 50$$
$$50 + 4 + 26 = 80$$
$$80 + 14 + 6 = 100$$

Lionel uses six addends in his story about acquiring rocks. To prove that his story totals 100, Lionel adds the 10 from the 14, the 39, and the 1 to get 50. He puts the 4 from the 14 in the "save box" so that he will remember to add it on later. He then adds 4, 26, and 50, and gets a total of 80. The 14 and 6 are combined with 80 to equal 100. Lionel used combinations of 10 (39 + 1 and 4 + 26) as well as multiples of 10 when planning his equation. His strategy of using the "save box" was shared by other students in his class.

Continued on next page

Ebony

"I'm wondering." Ebony said after reading the artical twice. May-be I could help these children by giving them something. Stufed animals? May-be thats the answer!"

The next day she told the teacher "Great! The howl class could help." She told the class to pich in animals. Ebony brought in 15, Anne 7, Sally 21, Rielly 23, Nina 19.

"Hey wait!" yelled Ebony we need a goal!" "100" "We need a few more."

I have a surprise said the teacher. She had 15 animals. "Yeah! yelled the class.

$$15 + 7 + 23 + 21 + 19 + 15$$
makes 100

Temara

Kelly and Kim collect stickers. Kelly had 38 stickers and Kim had 42 stickers. They asked there mom if they could buy more stickers. There mom said O.K.

The next day they took their money and went to the toy store. They bought 20 stickers! The end.

$$38 + 42 = 80$$
$$80 + 20 = 100$$

$$\begin{array}{r} 42 + \\ 38 \\ \hline 80 \end{array} \qquad \begin{array}{r} 80 + \\ 20 \\ \hline 100 \end{array}$$

Ebony's story is more elaborate than Laura's or Lionel's. Her theme and style are similar to that of "Emma's Animals." Ebony uses the numbers 15 + 7 + 23 + 21 + 19. These numbers easily combine into multiples of 5 and 10 and total 85. Ebony then knows that it's 15 more to get to 100.

Temara used only three addends in her 100 story. She chose two that totaled 80. Then she was able to add on 20 more to get to 100.

Addition and Subtraction Strategies

What Happens

Session 1: Introducing Comparing Situations
Students solve a comparing problem using their own strategies. They record their solutions so that someone else can understand them. Students share their strategies in a whole-group discussion.

Sessions 2 and 3: Capture 5 Students are introduced to the game Capture 5, which is played on the 100 chart. During Choice Time, students play Capture 5 and work on solving and creating word problems.

Sessions 4 and 5: Strategies for Combining
Students solve a combining problem. In a whole-class discussion they present their strategies. The class names each strategy. Choice Time continues with students solving additional word problems and playing Capture 5.

Session 6: Capture 5 Strategies Students discuss and compare strategies for playing Capture 5. Part of the discussion focuses on ways to calculate the total number of spaces moved. After the discussion, students solve a few Capture 5 equations. They then continue to work on Choice Time activities from the previous session.

Session 7: Strategies for Separating Students solve a separating problem. In a whole-class discussion they explain and compare their strategies, which are recorded on chart paper. As they did for combining strategies, they give names to each of these strategies. Choice Time continues with students solving additional story problems and playing Capture 5.

Session 8: How Far? Students solve problems about calculating the distance between two numbers on the 100 chart. They explain their solutions in writing. These problems are used as an assessment activity.

Mathematical Emphasis

- Developing strategies for comparing two quantities
- Calculating the distance between two numbers using the 100 chart
- Developing ways to approach different types of addition and subtraction situations
- Recognizing and solving problem structures with a variety of givens and unknowns
- Solving problems using numerical reasoning
- Recording and comparing solution strategies

What to Plan Ahead of Time

Materials

- Counters such as interlocking cubes or color tiles, buttons, or beans; and 100 charts (Sessions 1–8)
- Paste or glue sticks (Sessions 2–5)
- Hundred Number Wall Chart with number cards and translucent chart markers (Session 2–3, 6)

- Envelopes or resealable plastic bags: about 21 (Sessions 2–5)
- Markers for the 100 chart (transparent are best): 12 per pair of students (Sessions 2–8)
- Game pieces: 1 per student (Sessions 2–8)
- Chart paper (Sessions 4–7)
- Index cards: 2 per student (Sessions 6 and 7)

Continued on next page

What to Plan Ahead of Time (continued)

Other Preparation

■ Duplicate student sheets and teaching resources, located at the end of this unit, in the following quantities. If you have Student Activity Booklets, copy only the transparency marked with an asterisk.

For Session 1

Student Sheet 21, Comparing Story Problems (p. 178) or copies of problems you have created: 1 per student

Student Sheet 22, A Comparing Story Problem (p. 179): 1 per student (homework)

For Sessions 2–3

100 Chart (p. 190): 1 per pair, plus 1 per student (homework), plus 1 transparency* (optional)

Student Sheet 23, Capture 5 Recording Sheet (p. 180): 1 per student (class), plus 1 per student (homework)

Student Sheets 24 and 25, Change Cards (p. 181): 1 set per pair of students, plus 1 set per student (homework). You may want to copy the class sets on oaktag. Cut apart and store each classroom set in an envelope or resealable plastic bag.

Student Sheet 26, Capture 5 (p. 183): 1 per student (homework)

Story Problems, Set H (p. 187) or copies of problems you have created: 1 per student. If you are creating your own set of problems, use the same problem structures as those listed on page 115. Cut the sheets apart into individual problems. Store each problem in a separate envelope marked with its number. Paste an example of each problem on the front of each envelope.

For Sessions 4–5

Story Problems, Set I (p. 189) or copies of problems you have created: 1 per student. If you are creating your own set of problems, use the same problem structures as those listed on page 120. Prepare story problems as described under Sessions 2 and 3.

Student Sheet 8, Problem Strategies (p. 155): 1 per student (homework)

Student Sheet 9, Writing and Solving a Story Problem (p. 156): 1 per student (homework, as needed)

Student Sheet 22, A Comparing Story Problem (p. 179): 1 per student (homework, as needed)

Student Sheet 23, Capture 5 Recording Sheet (p. 180): 1 per student

For Session 6

Student Sheet 23, Capture 5 Recording Sheet (p. 180): 1 per student (homework)

Student Sheet 27, Capture 5 Equations (p. 184): 1 per student

For Session 7

Student Sheet 23, Capture 5 Recording Sheet (p. 180): 1 per student

Student Sheet 28, Alphabet Addition (p. 185): 1 per student (homework)

For Session 8

Student Sheet 29, How Far? (p. 186): 1 per student

■ Play a round or two of Capture 5 to familiarize yourself with the game. (Sessions 2–3)

Introducing Comparing Situations

Materials

- Counters
- Student Sheet 21 (1 per student)
- Student Sheet 22 (1 per student, homework)

What Happens

Students solve a comparing problem using their own strategies. They record their solutions so that someone else can understand them. Students share their strategies in a whole-group discussion. Their work focuses on:

- comparing two quantities
- recording strategies

Start-Up

Today's Number

Calendar Date *and* Number of School Days   Sometime during the school day, students generate expressions for Today's Number using subtraction and using only two numbers. For example, if the number is 134, possible solutions include: 164 – 30, 200 – 66, and 135 – 1. If you are counting the days in the school year, add another number to the class counting strip and fill in the next number on the blank 200 chart.

Activity

Problems About Comparing

Introduce a problem such as the one below to the whole class.

I'm going to read a problem for everyone to solve. I would like you to solve this problem in a way that makes sense to you. Use interlocking cubes or anything else you need. Remember, your job is to solve the problem and show how you solved it using words, pictures, and numbers. When everyone has finished, we will share strategies.

Kira and Jake are playing marbles. Kira has 40 marbles and Jake has 26. How many more marbles does Kira have than Jake?

Provide students with Student Sheet 21, Comparing Story Problems (or the problems you created). Students should have access to problem-solving materials. Students can work individually or in pairs, but each student records individually.

Remind students that their job is to solve the problem in a way that makes sense to them, check their solution, and record what they did so that someone else can understand. As you watch students work, continue to remind them to record clearly. Students who have time can do the second problem on the student sheet.

Some students will see this problem as a subtraction situation and "take away" 26 from 40. Others will see this as an "adding on" situation and count up from 26. See the **Teacher Note**, The Relationship Between Addition and Subtraction (p. 25).

Observing the Students

As you circulate, observe how students are approaching this comparing problem and note how they are recording their strategies for solving it.

- Are students adding on from 26 to 40 to calculate the difference? If so, do they add on by 1's, keeping track of the amount on their fingers or with tallies or cubes? Or do students add on by groups: 26, 36 (+ 10), 40 (+ 4)?

- Are students "taking away" either by counting backward by 1's or by groups from 40 to 26?

- Do students directly compare the two amounts by building a tower of 40 cubes and a tower of 26 cubes and counting the difference between the two?

The **Dialogue Box**, Counting On and Counting Back (p. 110), provides a variety of students' strategies for solving this comparing problem.

As you circulate, note the strategies students are using so that you can feature these during the discussion at the end of the session. Also pay attention to how comfortable students are dealing with these numbers. As with other problems in this unit, if numbers are too large (or small) for students, modify the problem to have smaller (or larger) numbers. When students finish, ask them to describe their solutions to a partner.

Sharing Strategies

Meet together as a class to share solution strategies. Use this time as an opportunity to model ways of recording a variety of solutions. For example, here are some solutions that students are likely to offer:

1. Counting up from 26 to 40 by 1's:

   27, 28, 29, 30, 31, 32, 33, 34, 35, 36, 37, 38, 39, 40. I used my fingers to keep track.

2. Counting up by 10's, then 1's:

   26 + 10 = 36
   36 + 4 = 40
   10 + 4 = 14

3. Counting back from 40 to 26 by 1's:

39, 38, 37, 36, 35, 34, 33, 32, 31, 30, 29, 28, 27, 26

One problem students frequently have with counting back (or on) by 1's is deciding which number to begin with. An example of this is in the **Dialogue Box,** Counting On and Counting Back (p. 110), where a student figures out the difference between 40 and 26 by counting backward.

4. Directly comparing the two amounts:

Students build towers of 40 and 26 cubes, then count the difference between the two towers. Or some students might build a tower of 40 cubes, break off 26, and count the amount left. This could be recorded as 40 − 26 = 14.

After several students have shared their approaches, ask:

Did anyone have a way that is different from one of the ways recorded?

Before the discussion ends, ask students to look at their own approach and decide which of the ones you recorded is closest to their own. Students can raise hands to say which approach they used. This is a way of validating all students' approaches and also giving you a sense of what kinds of strategies are being used in your class as a whole.

Session 1 Follow-Up

 **Homework**

A Comparing Story Problem   Ask students to think about a real situation where they might compare two amounts. For homework, students write and solve a story problem about comparing two quantities on Student Sheet 22. Students should be getting used to the requirement that they show their solution strategies with some combination of numbers, words, and pictures.

Types of Story Problems: Comparing

Earlier in this unit, students encountered two types of story problems: combining problems in which two quantities are combined to form a third quantity, and separating problems in which one quantity is removed from another, resulting in a portion of the original quantity.

Students are now introduced to a third type of story problem—comparing. In these problems, two quantities are compared to find the difference between them.

Chen has 12 marbles. John has 4. How many more marbles does Chen have than John? (Or how many fewer marbles does John have than Chen?)

The most familiar form of these problems is like this example: Two quantities are given, and the problem is to find the difference between them. However, comparing problems might also present one of the quantities and the difference:

Chen has 12 marbles. He has 8 more marbles than John. How many marbles does John have?

In this problem, one quantity is known (12 marbles), and the difference between the quantities is known (8 marbles). The problem requires finding a quantity that is 8 less than 12. Students often find comparison problems of this type more challenging than the first example because they must compare an unknown quantity with a known quantity. When students solve comparing problems of this type they may begin by choosing a number that might work, then adjust it until they achieve the required difference.

For example, consider problem 7 on Story Problems, Set H (p. 188):

> Jake and Kira each collected cans for recycling. Jake collected 48 cans in all. He collected 12 more than Kira. How many cans did Kira collect?

One student solved this problem by adding 12 to a number that was easy to manage.

Harris: I know 12 and 30 is 42. 12 and 31 is 43. I keep adding on: 12 + 32 is 44, 12 + 33 is 45, 12 + 34 is 46, 12 + 35 is 47, 12 + 36 is 48. So Kira had 36 cans.

While not an efficient method, Harris found a systematic strategy; he understands it and it works.

Counting On and Counting Back

In the activity Sharing Strategies (p. 107) these students are discussing the following problem:

> Kira and Jake are playing marbles. Kira has 40 marbles and Jake has 26. How many more marbles does Kira have than Jake?

The teacher encourages a variety of strategies for solving the problem and encourages students to think about how their strategy is similar to or different from strategies that are shared. At one point confusion arises over which numbers to include when counting back from 40.

Tim: I just counted up from 26 to 40. I said 26 to 30 is 4 and then it's 10 more to 40, so that's 14.

Did anyone else count up from 26 in a similar way as Tim? [*Four or five hands are raised.*]

Bjorn: I counted up, but I said 27, 28, 29, 30, 31, 32, 33, 34, 35, 36, 37, 38, 39, 40. And that's 14. [*As Bjorn counts he uses his fingers to keep track.*]

So you counted up from 26 to 40 by 1's and Tim counted up by groups. Bjorn, I was wondering how you knew what number to start counting from?

Bjorn: I thought of like when you play a game. When you move, you don't count the square you're on. First you move to the next square and that's one. So 27 is like one.

Temara: I did it like Tim, but I drew 26 marbles in red and then I just drew some more in blue until I had 40 in all.

How did you know how many more marbles Kira had than Jake?

Temara: The blue marbles were the extra ones. Up until 26 they had the same [number of marbles].

So it seems like a lot of people counted up in some way from 26 to 40. Raise your hand if you used that strategy. [*About three-quarters of the students raise their hands.*] **What strategy did the rest of you use?**

Lila: I took some away from the 40. I said 40 take away 10 is 30, so I wrote down 10. Then 30 take away 2 is 28, and I wrote down 2 with the 10. Then 28 take away 2 more. Then 10 and 2 and 2 is 14.

Interesting. Why did you take 2 away from the 30?

Lila: Because it's easier for me to take away by 2's to get to 26.

Angel: I just counted back from 40 and I used the number line but I got 15 not 14. I did 40, 39, 38, 37, 36, 35, 34, 33, 32, 31, 30, 29, 28, 27, 26. And that's 15. [*Angel demonstrates how she counted by pointing to each number on the number line posted in the classroom.*]

So you used the strategy of counting back by 1's. How did you decide where to start counting?

Angel: I counted the 40 because that was one of the extra marbles. Then I just kept going to 26.

Bjorn: That's sort of like what I did, but I counted up. I didn't count the 26 because it's like what I said about when you play a game. You don't count the number you're on.

Karina: I think that you either have to count the 40 or the 26, but you don't count both. That's why there was 1 extra.

Laura: If you think about where they are even, that's 26 because both people have 26 marbles. But then Kira has *more* than 26. So you don't count the 26; you count from 27 to 40.

So how does that work when you are counting backward? Both people don't have 40.

Laura: Right, so you count the 40, 39, 38 . . . but you don't count the 26.

Angel: This is confusing. I'm just not sure what you count.

Continued on next page

continued

Counting backward can sometimes be confusing. Deciding what to include in your count is one of the hard parts about counting. I'd like you to work with a partner and see if you can draw a picture or use the cubes to show how to count backward from 40 to 26. Then we'll discuss what you have done.

In this example the teacher decided to ask everyone to investigate what to include in the count by having students illustrate or build models of the problem to explain their thinking. This allowed students who seemed to have a clear idea of what to include to back up their thinking with an illustration. It also provided students who were unsure or confused the opportunity to make a concrete model of the problem and think about it in a different way.

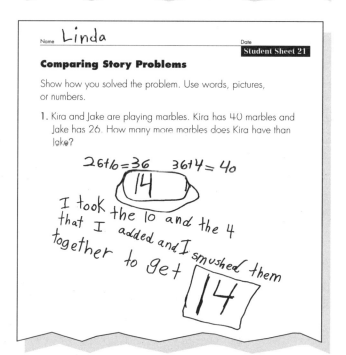

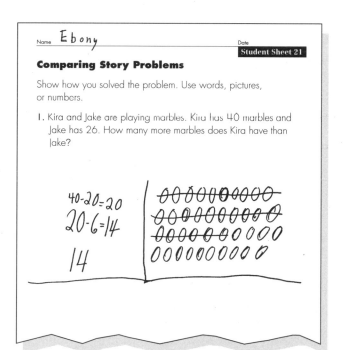

Capture 5

Materials

- 100 chart (1 per pair plus 1 per student for homework)
- Game markers (12 per pair)
- Game pieces (1 per student)
- Student Sheet 23 (1 per student, class; 1 per student, homework)
- Student Sheets 24 and 25 (1 per pair plus 1 per student, homework)
- Student Sheet 26 (1 per student, homework)
- Prepared envelopes containing Story Problems, Set H, cut apart
- Paste or glue sticks
- Overhead projector (optional)
- Transparency of 100 chart and transparent markers (optional)
- Hundred Number Wall chart with number cards and transluscent chart markers (optional)

What Happens

Students are introduced to the game Capture 5, which is played on the 100 chart. During Choice Time, students play Capture 5 and work on solving and creating word problems. Their work focuses on:

- operating with 1's and 10's on the 100 chart
- solving problems involving combining, separating, and comparing
- recording strategies for solving

Start-Up

Comparing Problems   At the beginning of class, talk with students about their experience writing comparing problems for homework. You might collect their problems and quickly look through them to get a sense of whether most students were able to come up with a comparing situation. Also note how students recorded their strategies.

Today's Number

Calendar Date *and* Number of School Days   Students generate story problems in which the answer is Today's Number. They can exchange problems and solve them as a way of checking. If you are counting the number of school days, add a number to the counting strip and fill in the next number on the blank 200 chart.

Activity

Introducing Capture 5

Capture 5 involves students in thinking about addition and subtraction of multiples of 10's and 1's. The game is played on the 100 chart. In order to capture a number, students move a game piece from one number on the chart to another, using Change Cards, Student Sheets 24 and 25. These cards include the numbers +1, −1, +2, −2, +3, −3, +10, −10, +20, −20, +30, and −30. By recording the moves, students see the combined effect of the changes on their starting number. For example, if a student is on 54 and wishes to capture 46, possible moves include:

$$54 - 10 + 2 = 46 \qquad 54 - 20 + 10 + 2 = 46 \qquad 54 + 3 - 1 - 10 = 46$$

The easiest way to introduce this game is to play a demonstration round with the class using a transparency of the 100 chart, so the gameboard is visible to all students. Or you may want to use the Hundred Number Wall Chart and translucent chart markers. Tape applied to paper squares can be used for game pieces.

This game is called Capture 5. To play, we use a 100 chart, a deck of Change Cards, 12 markers of one color, and a game piece for each player. You can play this game with partners or in teams.

To begin, we place 12 markers anywhere on the 100 chart, each marker on a different number. Each player puts a game piece on an empty square. Then each player is dealt five Change Cards.

If you are using the overhead, transparent markers are best so that students can see the numbers on the chart through them. Ask a volunteer to play a round with you. Deal five cards to each of you and arrange the remaining cards face down on a table. As you play, involve students in your turn.

This game is played by moving the game pieces around the board. The goal is to capture markers by landing on that square. Your Change Cards tell you what combinations of moves you can make. You can use one card or up to all five cards to determine your moves.

Show students your Change Cards, or write the numbers on the board. Explain that addition cards move game markers forward on the 100 chart and subtraction cards move markers backward. For example, if play begins on the number 54, and cards –10 and +2 are used, the game piece would jump back 10, then forward 2, and land on 46. A game marker on 46 would be captured.

Looking at the cards together with the class, ask students to suggest one or more cards that could be used so your game piece will land on a square with a marker. Record suggestions on the chalkboard in equation form:

$$54 - 10 + 2 = 46$$

$$54 + 2 - 10 = 46$$

Move your game piece to the square indicated by the cards selected. If there is a marker on the square, remove it from the board and tell students it has been captured. Explain that a player can capture only one marker during a turn and it must be the last square the game piece lands on.

Once a move has been made, the turn is over. Used Change Cards are placed face down in a discard pile. Replacement cards are taken from the deck. After the whole deck has been used, the discard pile is shuffled and placed face down again.

Continue playing the demonstration game by looking together with the class at your opponent's cards. Talk about which cards could be combined so the game piece lands on a square with a marker. Record the cards suggested in equation form on the chalkboard, then move the game piece.

Play the game for a few more rounds, or until students understand how to play. Continue taking turns using their Change Cards to move the game pieces around the gameboard. The first player to capture 5 markers wins.

These are additional rules for Capture 5:

- If you *can* move, you *must* move, whether or not you can capture a marker. You choose how many of your Change Cards you want to use.

- If you *cannot* move, put all Change Cards in the discard pile and take all new ones. That becomes a turn. You cannot move until your next turn.

Depending on how much time is left in the session, you may want to have everyone in the class play a game of Capture 5. Students can play in pairs or in teams. Having teams encourages conversation among team members about possible moves. Provide each pair or group with the materials they need to play. (**Note:** The game markers students use must fit inside the squares of the 100 chart.) Players should record equations on paper as they play. Circulate and observe students, to be sure that they understand the rules.

Post the following list of choices on the board or chart paper:

> 1. Capture 5
>
> 2. Solving Story Problems

Choice 1: Capture 5

Materials: 100 chart; Student Sheet 23, Capture 5 Recording Sheet; deck of Change Cards; 12 markers of one color (markers must fit inside the squares of the 100 chart); 2 game pieces (one per player)

Students (or teams) take turns trying to capture game markers by moving their game piece on the 100 chart. They use Change Cards to determine how far they can move. The object of the game is to collect 5 markers. As they play they record their moves on the Capture 5 Recording Sheet.

Choice 2: Solving Story Problems

Materials: Prepared envelopes with Story Problems, Set H, cut apart; paste or glue sticks

Students are familiar with Solving Story Problems from previous sessions. Explain that they should solve a few problems each day. Because students will be recording their strategies in a way that is clear and understandable to others, they will probably be able to complete no more than three problems in each session.

Story Problems, Set H, consists of different types of story problems. Make sure that students are trying a variety of problem structures. Problem Set H includes the following problem structures:

Problem 1: comparing

Problem 2: combining 3 addends

Problem 3: multi-step problem
(combining and separating)

Problem 4: separating

Problem 5: multi-step problem
(combining and separating)

Problem 6: separating

Problem 7: comparing

Problem 8: separating

Observing the Students

Use the following questions as a guide as you observe and monitor students.

Capture 5

■ How are students planning their moves? Do they figure out how many spaces they need to move, then try to find a combination of Change Cards that will work, or do they randomly select cards and move that amount?

■ Do some students always count by 1's? Watch them and see whether they begin to move vertically by multiples of 10 as well as horizontally by 1's. Talk with students who are moving vertically: How do they know a vertical jump is the same as +10 or –10? Can they prove it? Is it always true? How do they know?

As you watch students play, ask questions such as:

■ **You used your –10 and your –2 to move from 56 to 44. How far back did you move?**

■ **You just jumped from 33 to 43, then to 53. How far did you move? How do you know it's 20?**

■ **I see you recorded one of your moves here as 14 – 1 + 2 + 20 = 35. If you moved by 1's from 14 to 35, how many moves would it take? Why do you think so?**

You'll probably need to remind students to record their moves. Recording can be difficult in this game, because in the excitement of making a capture, students forget where they started and what cards they used. If teams are playing, one student can record as the other moves. Or tell students to put the Change Cards they are using near their recording sheet so they can record the equation after they move.

All students should play Capture 5 during these two sessions. Students who seem to have a firm grasp of this game can be introduced to the variations Capture More, Capture 3, or Capture All in later sessions.

Variations

■ **Capture 3:** Capturing 3 markers wins.

■ **Capture More:** Play continues until all markers have been captured. The player with the most markers wins.

■ **Capture All:** Play this version cooperatively or as a solitaire game. Try to capture all markers on the board in as few turns as possible. You may use one or two game pieces. You may move a single game piece during a turn or split moves between the two pieces. *Each* piece that ends up on a marker captures it, so it is possible to capture more than one marker on a turn. (Since this version requires separate recording for each game piece, it is best not to record during this version.)

Solving Story Problems

- Are students able to make sense out of each type of problem situation? If not, note which problem structure they have difficulty with. You may want to work with small groups of students on certain types of problems. Or if the majority of the class is having difficulty, discuss strategies for solving that problem type.

- Are students recording their solutions in ways that allow you to understand their strategies? If you don't understand what has been recorded, tell students which part you can follow and which is confusing. You can also ask students to show you their strategies, then ask them to add to or revise what they've written so it truly reflects how they solved the problem. Sometimes as students explain what they did, they realize what is missing in the way they recorded their solutions. After two students have solved the same problem, ask them to explain their strategies to each other.

Note: Students should save one completed version of Student Sheet 23, Capture 5 Recording Sheet for a discussion during Session 6.

Sessions 2 and 3 Follow-Up

Capture 5   After Session 3, students play Capture 5 with someone at home. Each student will need the following: 100 chart; Student Sheets 24 and 25, Change Cards; Student Sheet 26, Capture 5; and Student Sheet 23, Capture 5 Recording Sheet. Discuss what objects students could use at home for markers (pennies, beans, etc.). Change Cards can be cut apart at home.

 **Homework**

Strategies for Combining

Materials

- Prepared envelopes containing Story Problems, Set I, cut apart
- Paste or glue sticks
- Chart paper
- Counters
- Student Sheet 8 (1 per student, homework)
- Student Sheet 9 (1 per student, homework)
- Student Sheet 22 (1 per student, homework)
- Student Sheet 23 (1 per student)

What Happens

Students solve a combining problem. In a whole-class discussion they present their strategies. The class names each strategy. Choice Time continues with students solving additional word problems and playing Capture 5. Their work focuses on:

- describing and comparing strategies for combining

Start-Up

Capture 5   Students discuss their experience playing Capture 5 with someone at home.

Today's Number

Calendar Date _and_ Number of School Days   Have students spend 5 minutes generating expressions for Today's Number. They can exchange papers with partners and check each other's work. Then ask students to think about how far away from a certain number Today's Number is. For example, if you are using the calendar date and the number is 12, some questions might be: How far is 12 from 30? from 50? from 75? from 100? If the number is larger, say, 135, questions might include: How far is 135 from 100? from 150? from 200? from 173?

If you are counting the number of school days, add another number to the counting strip and fill in the next number on the blank 200 chart.

Activity

Solving a Combining Problem

Write the following story problem on the chalkboard.

> Kira and Jake were playing Cover-Up. Jake covered 19 buttons. Kira counted 24 buttons that were not covered. How many buttons did they have in all?

Read the problem with students and ask them to imagine the problem, then describe the situation. Once you are sure students can visualize the problem, they can begin to work.

As students work on this problem, they record at least two ways to solve it. Remind them to use words, numbers, and/or pictures to explain their strategy. As students finish, put them together into groups of three or four to explain their strategies to each other.

The Combining Poster: Comparing Solutions

For this discussion you will be making a poster of the different strategies students used to solve the combining problem. At the top of the poster, write a brief version of the problem in words. As students explain their strategies, record them below the problem. (You may want to record the strategies on chart paper and copy them onto a more permanent poster later, since there may be changes as the discussion goes on.) So that you and the students have a way to refer to different strategies, write a number beside each strategy. See the **Teacher Notes**, Students' Addition and Subtraction Strategies (p. 32) and Developing Numerical Strategies (p. 33), for information about common strategies.

After the first strategy, ask each student who volunteers a solution strategy to explain it and indicate whether it is the same as or different from one(s) already recorded. You might want to write students' names next to the ways they chose to solve the problem. For examples of the dialogue in one classroom, see the **Dialogue Box**, How Many Buttons? (p. 122).

When all strategies have been recorded, have students compare their strategies to those on the poster. First talk through the strategies on the poster, reminding students that these are strategies offered by different students to solve the same problem.

Look at the first strategy I've written on the poster. I think Karina and Lionel both did it this way. They started with 19 and then counted up by tens, 29, 39, and then counted on four, 40, 41, 42, 43. Who else solved the problem by counting up by tens?

Let's look at the second strategy. Can anyone explain this way?

There will probably be some student strategies that are virtually the same as those on the poster, with just a slight variation. You do not need to record every variation on the poster as long as you have all of the basic approaches being used in your class, but do have students explain how their approaches vary:

Rosie: Mine is like the first way because I counted up by 10's but I started at the 24 and said 34, 44, that's 20, so take away 1 because I only need to count up 19. So the answer is 43.

Ask students to help you think of a name or phrase that describes each strategy, so you'll have a short way to refer to them other than "the first strategy" and "the second strategy." For example, "count up by 10's, count up by 1's" might describe the "strategy" used by Lionel and Karina.

Some strategies may be easy to describe this way; others may not be. Don't force names or phrases that don't make sense to the students. The idea is to think of something that reminds everyone of that approach. It's not necessary to come up with a phrase for every strategy on the poster. Hang the poster in a visible place so that students can refer to it over time.

19 buttons covered. 24 buttons not covered. How many buttons in all?

$$19 + 24$$

1. $19 + 20 = 39$ $19 + 10 = 29$
   $39 + 4 = 43$ $29 + 10 = 39$
                           $39 + 4 = 43$

2. $19 + 24$
   10 9
   $24 + 10 = 34$
   $34 + 9 = 43$

3. |||||||||||||||||
   |||||||||||||||||||||||||||

   count all

4.   19
   $+24$
     $30 + 13$

     $30 + 13 = 43$

5. $10 + 20 = 30$
   $9 + \ 4 = 13$
   $30 + 13 = 43$

A combining poster

Collect each student's work for this problem so that you can get a sense of how the class as a whole is solving combining problems. Explain to students that you will return these papers for them to put into their math folders.

For the remainder of this session, students continue to work on Capture 5 and Solving Story Problems. Add Story Problems, Set I, to the collection of story problems for those students who are ready. Remind students that it is not necessary for them to complete every story problem, but instead it is important that they fully explain their solutions using words, numbers, and pictures for the problems they do work on. Story Problems, Set I, contains these problem types:

Choice Time

Problem 1: combining

Problem 4: separating

Problem 2: comparing

Problem 5: comparing

Problem 3: combining with
unknown change

Problem 6: multi-step problem
(combining and separating)

Sessions 4 and 5 Follow-Up

Solving Story Problems   After Session 4, students choose a problem or two that they have not done to work on at home. They glue or staple the problem(s) they choose onto Student Sheet 8, Problem Strategies.

Solving More Story Problems   After Session 5, students make up, illustrate, and solve a story problem of their choice. Students record their work on Student Sheet 9, Writing and Solving a Story Problem, or on Student Sheet 22, A Comparing Story Problem, depending on the type of problem (addition or subtraction or comparing) they choose to write. The class can collect these in a class book for further work.

Writing Story Problems   You might want to write a few story problems that have to do with a book your class is reading or a topic you are studying, or you might have some students write the stories and then others can solve them.

In this discussion the teacher is recording strategies for solving the following problem:

> Kira and Jake were playing Cover-Up. Jake covered 19 buttons. Kira counted 24 buttons that were not covered. How many buttons did they have in all?

As students explain their strategies, the teacher records them, then asks students to think about whether they solved the problem in a similar way.

Simon: I added 19 to 24.

How did you do it?

Simon: I know 24 is 20 plus 4, so I added 20 to 19. That's 39. Then I added the 4. That's 43.

[*The teacher writes*]   19 + 20 = 39
                          39 + 4 = 43

Simon, does this show your strategy? Did anyone else use a way similar to Simon's?

Laura: Well, I added on the 20 by 10's. 19 plus 10 is 29; 29 plus 10 is 39. Then 4 more is 43.

You broke apart the 24 into 10 plus 10 plus 4.

Phoebe: I did it a little different. I added the 19 to the 24. Like I went 10 plus 9 is 19, so 24 plus 10 is 34, then add the 9 to the 34.

[*The teacher records*]

   19 + 24   24 + 10 = 34   34 + 9 = 43
      /\
  10 + 9

These strategies are similar. Each person broke apart one of the numbers into smaller numbers—in each case a multiple of 10—that were easier to work with. Any more strategies?

Franco: I drew 24 lines in a row. Then I drew 19 and then I counted 19 and 24 and got 43.

[*The teacher draws 24 vertical lines and then 19 vertical lines.*]

Did you count all of them?

Franco: Yes.

[*The teacher writes "counted all" under Franco's vertical lines.*]

Paul: I built towers of 19 cubes and 24 cubes, then I put them together and counted them.

[*The teacher adds "Paul used cubes and counted all" to Franco's strategy.*]

Juanita: I wrote the problem 19 plus 24 going up and down.

Like this? [*The teacher records the problem using vertical notation.*]

          19
         +24

Juanita: Well, first I added the 9 and 4 and got 13. Then I added the 2 and 1 and got 30. [*Juanita shows her written work.*]:

          19
         +24
         313

But I knew it couldn't be this high a number. So then I did 30 plus 13 and got 43.

[*The teacher writes*]   19
                           +24
                         30 + 13 = 43

Juanita: You can't put the 13 below the line. It's too big. You have to do something like borrow.

Yes, you have to do something with the 13.

Jeffrey: The 1 goes over here with the other 10's.

Juanita's way works because this helps her remember that this is 30, not 3. [*The teacher points to the tens column.*]

Bjorn: I did 10 plus 20 is 30, and then 4 plus 9 is 13, and 30 plus 13 is 43.

[*The teacher records*] 10 + 20 = 30
                          4 + 9 = 13
                         30 + 13 = 43

Juanita: Hey, that's sort of like me!

Juanita's way of solving the problem and Bjorn's way are similar. They just recorded and kept track of their thinking in different ways.

Capture 5 Strategies

What Happens

Students discuss and compare strategies for playing Capture 5. Part of the discussion focuses on ways to calculate the total number of spaces moved. After the discussion, students solve a few Capture 5 equations. They then continue to work on Choice Time activities from the previous session. Their work focuses on:

- calculating the distance between two numbers on the 100 chart
- reducing an equation with multiple addends to one with only two addends
- solving problems involving combining, separating, and comparing

Start-Up

Story Problems   Have students copy the problem they wrote for homework onto index cards. Explain that these problems will be available for other students to solve during the next Choice Time (Session 7). Collect students' original problems and solutions and put them together in a book. Your class might enjoy trading story problems with another second or third grade class.

Today's Number

Calendar Date *and* Number of School Days   Students express Today's Number by writing equations with a missing part. For example, if the calendar date is 29, one equation might be 23 + ____ = 29 or 50 − ____ = 29. Record a student's equation on chart paper and have other students figure out the solution. If you are counting the number of days in the year, add the next number to the counting strip and fill in another number on the blank 200 chart.

Materials

- Index cards (1 per student)
- Students' completed Student Sheet 23 (from Sessions 2 and 3)
- Hundred Number Wall Chart with number cards
- Chart paper
- Counters
- Student Sheet 23 (1 per student, homework, optional)
- Student Sheet 27 (1 per student)

Visualizing the 100 Chart

This activity focuses on sharing strategies that students developed as they played Capture 5. They will also examine some of their equations from Capture 5 and try to rewrite some of them.

Ask students to get one completed copy of Student Sheet 23, Capture 5 Recording Sheet. Then display the Hundred Number Wall Chart with numbers in place. Seat students around the chart so everyone can see it.

Pretend that you are a butterfly that has just landed on number 34 on our 100 Chart. What numbers are on either side of you? (33 and 35) **Now pretend you are looking up. What number is above you?** (24) **and what number is below you?** (44)

The numbers above and below may be confusing to some students. You may want to explain that *above* means "one row up" and *below* means "one row down."

Next have students close their eyes and imagine a 100 chart in their minds. Ask them to imagine the number 24 and think about the numbers on either side of 24 and above and below 24.

Now ask them to imagine another number on the 100 chart.

OK, open your eyes for a minute and look at the 100 chart again. This time I'm going to ask you to think about another number. I'll ask you to close your eyes and imagine it on the 100 chart. Try to think about what numbers are nearby the number, just like we did with the number 24.

Have students close their eyes (or cover up the chart or turn off the overhead projector) and imagine the number 47 on the 100 chart. Ask students what numbers are next to 47. What numbers are above or below 47? You might also ask them to imagine what number is two rows down from 47 or three rows up.

After each number, encourage students to explain their strategy for knowing the location of certain numbers. Listen for explanations that demonstrate understanding that numbers above and below a target number are 10 more or 10 less than the target number. Also take note of how comfortable students are at predicting numbers that are "three rows up" or "two rows over."

Visualizing the 100 chart may be a challenging task for some second graders. You may want to have some students find the answers to these questions by looking at the 100 chart instead of closing their eyes.

The 100 chart is an important tool and representation of the numbers in our number system. Understanding how it is organized and where numbers are in relationship to one another is a step in understanding more about numbers and their relationships. Students can try this activity with a partner or in small groups at various times throughout the school day or year.

Focus students' attention on the game Capture 5.

Strategies for Playing Capture 5

For the last few math sessions you have been playing Capture 5. Suppose you were playing Capture 5, you were on the number 34, and you wanted to capture a marker on the number 56. Using the Change Cards, what cards could get you to this number?

You may want to identify the two target numbers (34 and 56) on the large 100 chart in some way so that students remember what they are. You may also need to review what the values of the Change Cards are (plus/minus 1, 2, 3; plus/minus 10, 20, 30). Write these values on the board if necessary.

As students suggest possible combinations for moving from 34 to 56, record them on the board in the form of an equation.

$$34 + 10 + 10 + 2 = 56$$
$$34 + 3 + 20 - 1 = 56$$
$$34 + 30 - 3 - 2 - 3 = 56$$
$$34 - 10 + 30 + 2 = 56$$
$$34 + 1 + 1 + 20 = 56$$

When you were playing Capture 5, how did you think about which marker to capture and what combinations of cards to use?

Some students, after playing Capture 5 over a number of days, have very clear plans or strategies for moving on the 100 chart. They may be easily combining positive and negative numbers. Other students may use more of a trial-and-error approach. This initial discussion can give you a sense of how students are approaching this game.

One question that you will be interested in for all students is whether they are able to calculate the total number of spaces moved between two numbers.

Let's look at these equations for getting from 34 to 56 and let's also look at the 100 chart. I'm interested in figuring out the total number of spaces you had to move to get from 34 to 56.

As students offer ideas, record them on chart paper. As with any problem, there will be a range of strategies. You may notice that some students do not see the connection between a Capture 5 equation for this problem and their strategies for calculating the distance between 34 and 56. For example, some students might have no difficulty making up this Capture 5 equation using Change Cards: $34 + 10 + 10 + 2 = 56$. But when asked how far it is between 34 and 56, they solve this problem by counting up from 34 by 1's.

You can help to bridge these two strategies by focusing students' attention on the different parts of the Capture 5 equation.

Rosie found that the distance between 34 and 56 is 22. She moved a total of 22 spaces on the 100 chart in order to capture a marker that was on 56. Here's an equation that we came up with that also shows how Rosie might have moved in order to capture the marker on 56:

$$34 + 10 + 10 + 2 = 56$$

Where in this equation does it show that Rosie moved a total of 22 spaces?

If students do not seem to understand this question, you might begin by asking them what each component means. For example, "What does the 34 tell you? What does the 56 tell you? What kinds of moves did Rosie make?"

Another way of writing this equation is $34 + \_\_\_\_\_ = 56$. Suppose we were not using Change Cards but instead we just wanted to put one number in the blank. What would it be and how do you know?

Choose another equation students generated that represents how to get from 34 to 56 using the Change Cards. For now, choose an equation that uses only positive Change Cards, such as the following:

$$34 + 1 + 1 + 20 = 56$$

Here's another equation from our list, which shows the moves you could make with Change Cards to get from 34 to 56. Where in this equation does it show the total number of spaces moved?

In this equation, the 22 spaces were moved by making a move of 1, another move of 1, and then a move of 20. So altogether that's a move of 22 spaces.

Circle $+ 1 + 1 + 20$ so that students see the total of 22.

Consider focusing only on equations that use positive Change Cards. While some students may be able to see that in the equation $34 - 10 + 30 + 2 = 56$, the moves $-10 + 30 + 2$ result in a total of 22, this is not easy for most second graders to understand, especially as the equation begins with a negative number.

Note: If you feel that some students are ready to work with positive and negative change, make additional equations for them that involve these sorts of moves. Or you could have them use the equations they have generated on their Capture 5 Recording Sheet, many of which will probably use positive and negative change, and calculate the total distance moved.

Calculating How Far

Distribute Student Sheet 27, Capture 5 Equations, to each student and explain that these are some equations from a Capture 5 game. Their job is to look at each equation and figure out the total number of spaces moved. Under each example, students should rewrite the equation using only two addends. For example, if the equation were 28 + 2 + 10 + 20 + 3 = 63, students would write 28 + 35 = 63.

Students should be encouraged to work with partners, but each student completes a separate student sheet.

Observing the Students

As students are working, circulate around the classroom to get an idea of how easy or difficult this task is for them. Take note of the following:

■ How do students calculate the total distance from one number to another? Do they use the Capture 5 equation? Do they use the 100 chart?

■ Are students able to rewrite an equation using only two addends, and can they tell you where in the Capture 5 equation the second addend comes from?

When students are finished, if there is time they can continue to work on choices from the previous session. You may want to encourage some students to play Capture 5 and to think about some of the strategies for moving that were discussed earlier. As students capture markers on the board, ask them to figure out how many spaces they moved in all.

Session 6 Follow-Up

More Capture 5 Students play Capture 5 with someone at home. They should already have directions and 100 charts at home from a previous homework assignment. Students can make their own recording sheet (or give each student a copy of Student Sheet 23).

 **Homework**

Strategies for Separating

What Happens

Students solve a separating problem. In a whole-class discussion they explain and compare their strategies, which are recorded on chart paper. As they did for combining strategies, they give names to each of these strategies. Choice Time continues with students solving additional story problems and playing Capture 5. Their work focuses on:

■ describing, recording, and comparing strategies for a separating problem

Start-Up

Today's Number

Calendar Date and Number of School Days   Have each student spend 5 minutes generating expressions for Today's Number. Students exchange papers with partners and check each other's work. Then ask students to think about how far away from a certain number Today's Number is. For example, if you are using the calendar date and the number is 14, some questions might be: How far is 14 from 30? from 50? from 75? from 100? If the number is larger than, say, 145, questions might include: How far is 145 from 100? from 150? from 200? from 173? If you are counting the number of school days, add a card to the class counting strip and fill in another number on the blank 200 chart.

Materials

- Chart paper
- Index cards (1 per student and a few extras)
- Counters
- Materials for Solving Story Problems (from Sessions 2, 3, and 4)
- Story problems written by students (Session 5, homework)
- Student Sheet 23 (1 per student)
- Student Sheet 28 (1 per student, homework)

Activity

Solving a Separating Problem

In this session, students solve a separating problem, then come together as a class to discuss and compare their strategies. During the discussion their strategies for solving separating problems are recorded on a class poster.

Write the following story problem on the chalkboard:

> Jake had 35¢ in his pocket. 17¢ dropped out through a hole in his pocket. How much money did he have left?

As students work on this problem, they record at least two ways to solve it. When students finish, put them together into groups of three or four to explain their strategies to each other.

For this discussion you will be making a poster of the different strategies students used to solve the above problem. At the top of the poster, write a brief version of the problem in words; for example:

> 35¢ in Jake's pocket. 17¢ dropped out. How much is left?
> 35 – 17

Explain to students that you will be making a poster for this problem the way you did for the combining problem.

As students offer strategies, record them below the problem. (You may want to record the strategies on chart paper and copy them onto a more permanent poster later, since there may be changes as the discussion goes on.) So that you and the students have a way to refer to different strategies, write a number beside each strategy.

As each student describes a strategy, encourage him or her to explain which of the recorded strategies it matches or to identify it as a new strategy that needs to be recorded. Don't worry if some of the strategies also appeared on the combining poster; in fact, some students may want to comment on similarities between the two posters.

Ask students how they can write the problem and its solution in numbers. Don't be surprised if students express this problem as both addition and subtraction. For example, one second grader thought about this problem as 35 – 17. He solved it by counting backward by 1's starting at 34, and he kept track of the 17 on his fingers. Another student first subtracted 10 from 35 and got 25, then subtracted 7 from 25 to get 18.

Other students used addition to solve this problem. Some used the equation 17 + ___ = 35 in their solution. Most of these students counted on either by 1's or by 10's and 1's from 17 to 35. Regardless of whether they used addition or subtraction, students had a clear image of what the problem was asking and used strategies that made sense to them.

As students offer their strategies, it will be important for them to see the equation written in both horizontal and vertical form:

$$35 - 17 = 18 \qquad 17 + 18 = 35 \qquad \begin{array}{r} 35 \\ -17 \\ \hline 18 \end{array} \qquad \begin{array}{r} 17 \\ +18 \\ \hline 35 \end{array}$$

When all strategies have been recorded, ask students to help you think of a name or phrase that describes each strategy in much the same way you did for the combining poster. Hang the separating poster along with the combining poster in a visible place in the classroom and encourage students to examine them more closely later.

These posters have many good strategies for solving combining and separating problems. Some of you might want to try a strategy for solving a combining or separating problem that is different from the one you used to solve the problem. I also know that some of you have more than one strategy for solving these types of problems. See if you can find them on the posters.

Collect each student's work for this problem so that you can get a sense of how the class as a whole is solving separating problems. Explain to students that you will return these papers for them to put in their math folders.

Activity

Choice Time

For the remainder of this session, students continue to work on Capture 5 and Solving Story Problems. Students can solve story problems from any student sheet not done previously. You can also make available problems that students wrote for homework after Session 5. Students can borrow a card, copy the problem, and solve it. When they are finished, they can ask the author to check their work.

As students are working on problems, try to get a sense of how comfortable they are with the strategies they're using. Some students may be ready to refine their strategies in some way, and others may have commented on a particular strategy during the discussion but not yet tried to solve a problem using that strategy. See the **Teacher Note,** Moving from 1's to Groups (p. 94), for an example of how one teacher supported a student as he refined his strategy for combining numbers.

Session 7 Follow-Up

Alphabet Addition   Students work with a system in which letters of the alphabet are worth 5, 10, or 15. They determine how much 5 different words are worth and record them on Student Sheet 28, Alphabet Addition.

How Far?

What Happens

Students solve problems about calculating the distance between two numbers on the 100 chart. They explain their solutions in writing. These problems are used as an assessment activity. Their work focuses on:

■ using multiples of 10 and 1's to find the difference between two numbers

Start-Up

Today's Number

Calendar Date *and* **Number of School Days**   Students generate expression for Today's Number using subtraction and using only two numbers. For example, if the number is 142, possible solutions include: 162 – 20, 200 – 58, and 143 – 1. If you are counting the number of school days, add a card to the class counting strip and fill in another number on the blank 200 chart.

Materials

■ Student Sheet 29 (1 per student)

■ 100 charts and counters

Activity

In the last few math sessions you have been playing the game Capture 5 and we have been talking about your strategies for solving addition and subtraction problems. Today you will solve two problems that involve figuring out how far away one number is from another.

Distribute Student Sheet 29, How Far?, to each student. Explain to students that you would like to get an idea about how each of them is thinking about these problems and that for this activity each person should work alone.

Briefly go over both problems on the student sheet. You may need to remind students to explain their thinking using words and numbers.

When you are explaining your thinking for each problem, it is important to use words and numbers so that someone reading your paper can understand how you figured out the distance between two numbers.

Counters and 100 charts should be available. Remind students to include these tools in their explanation if they use them.

Assessment

How Far?

As you watch students work, make notes about the following questions:

- Which students can solve these problems fluently using numerical reasoning, without consulting a 100 chart?
- Which students count by 1's to find the distance between the two points on the 100 chart? Which students are using 10 and multiples of 10 in their solutions?
- How clearly are students able to record their solutions? Do their explanations convey their thinking?

Let students who need additional challenge answer this question on the back of the student sheet: Suppose you had a chart that went above 100. You're on 123 and you want to get to 98. How far is it? What about from 139 to 161?

As students finish, collect their papers so that you can look at them more closely. The **Teacher Note**, Assessment: How Far? (p. 133), provides some examples of second graders' solutions to these problems and offers suggestions for looking at this set of papers.

Activity

Choosing Student Work to Save

As the unit ends, you may want to use one of the following options for creating a record of students' work on this unit.

- Students look back through their folders and think about what they learned in this unit, what they remember most, and what was hard or easy for them. You might have students discuss this with partners or in the whole group.
- Depending on how you organize and collect student work, you may want to have students select some examples of their work to keep in a math portfolio. In addition, you may want to choose some examples from each student's folder to include. Items such as story problems; the two assessment tasks, Solving a Problem About 100 and How Far?; and work on Today's Number can be useful pieces for assessing student growth over the school year.
- Send a selection of work home for families to see. Students can write a cover letter describing their work in this unit. This work should be returned if you are keeping a year-long portfolio of mathematics work for each student.

Assessment: How Far?

In the assessment activity How Far?, students are asked to determine the difference between two numbers. They explain their strategies in writing so that they are clear to someone else. Look at how students approach these two problems to get a sense of the strategies they are using, particularly which students count by 1's from one number to the other and which students are using groups of 10's and 1's to determine the difference. The following are examples of student work for the problem: How far is it from 38 to 65?

Trini and Olga both counted by 1's from 38 to 65. One used the 100 chart and the other her fingers as tools for solving this problem. They are clear about where to start and which numbers to include in their count.

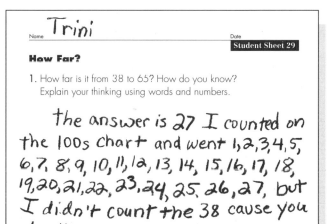

Name **Trini**   Date
How Far?   Student Sheet 29

1. How far is it from 38 to 65? How do you know? Explain your thinking using words and numbers.

the answer is 27 I counted on
the 100s chart and went 1,2,3,4,5,
6,7, 8,9, 10, 11, 12, 13, 14, 15, 16, 17, 18,
19,20,21,22, 23,24, 25, 26,27, but
I didn't count the 38 cause you
don't in the real game.

Name **Olga**   Date
    Student Sheet 29
How Far?

1 How far is it from 38 to 65? How do you know? Explain your thinking using words and numbers.

I got it by counted on my figers.
I started at 39 and I counted
to 65.
  I got 27.

A next step for Trini and Olga might be to help them begin to use "chunks" of numbers as they count from one number to another. For example, questions such as "How far is it from 38 to 40? from 40 to 50?" might be one way of developing this idea of counting by bigger groups. See the **Teacher Note**, Moving from 1's to Groups (p. 94), for more information and an example of a dialogue between student and teacher about counting by larger groups.

Continued on next page

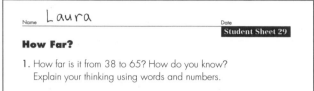

Name __Laura__   Date
Student Sheet 29

How Far?

1. How far is it from 38 to 65? How do you know?
   Explain your thinking using words and numbers.

I was on 38
and I went bellow 38 and I was on
48 I went bellow 48 and I was on
58 I went bellow 58 and I was on
68 I went back 3 and got 33

Name __Karina__   Date
Student Sheet 29

How Far?

1. How far is it from 38 to 65? How do you know?
   Explain your thinking using words and numbers.

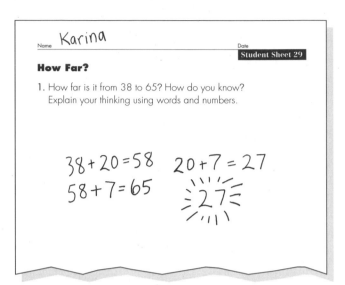

$38 + 20 = 58$ $20 + 7 = 27$
$58 + 7 = 65$ 27

Name __Jess__   Date
Student Sheet 29

How Far?

1. How far is it from 38 to 65? How do you know?
   Explain your thinking using words and numbers.

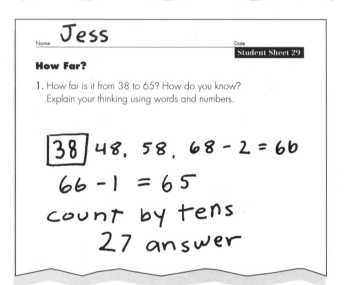

$\boxed{38}$ 48, 58, 68 $- 2 = 66$
$66 - 1 = 65$
count by tens
27 answer

Karina also counted up from 38, but she did so in
two steps using a group of 20 and then a group
of 7. This is a consistent strategy for Karina, one
that she uses for both addition and subtraction.

Name __Angel__   Date
Student Sheet 29

How Far?

1. How far is it from 38 to 65? How do you know?
   Explain your thinking using words and numbers.

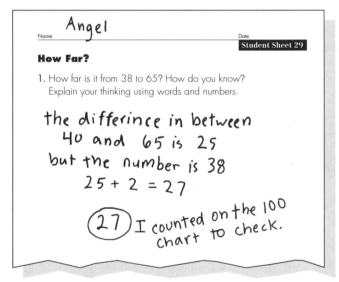

the differince in between
40 and 65 is 25
but the number is 38
$25 + 2 = 27$
27 I counted on the 100
chart to check.

Laura and Jess counted up from 38 using groups
of 10. Both students added on three 10's and
then subtracted 3 or "went back," as Laura
explained, to get to the target number of 65.
However, Laura seems confused by what "going
back" means, adding on 3 to the 30 to get 33
instead of subtracting to get the answer of 27.
This is a common confusion, especially when students are playing Capture 5 on the 100 chart.
Issues of directionality are still slippery ideas
for young students. They benefit from talking
through their strategies and demonstrating their
ideas with each other and in the whole group in
order to solidify their thinking.

Angel adjusted the problem a bit in order to
work with a multiple of 10. She mentally knew
that the difference between 40 and 65 is 25. She
then added 2 more to compensate for the difference between 40 and 38. Angel seems to know a
lot about numbers and their relationship to each
other. Many students get to this point and are
unsure whether to add the 2 or subtract it.

Today's Number

Today's Number is one of three routines that are built into the grade 2 *Investigations* curriculum. Routines provide students with regular practice in important mathematical ideas such as number combinations, counting and estimating data, and concepts of time. For Today's Number, which is done daily (or most days), students write equations that equal the number of days they have been in school. Each day, the class generates ways to make that number. For example, on the tenth day of school, students look for ways to combine numbers and operations to make 10.

This routine gives students an opportunity to explore some important ideas in number. By generating ways to make the number of the day, they explore:

■ number composition and part-whole relationships (e.g., 10 can be $4 + 6$, $5 + 5$, or $20 - 10$)

■ equivalent arithmetical expressions

■ different operations

■ ways of deriving new numerical expressions by systematically modifying prior ones (e.g., $5 + 5 = 10$, so $5 + 6 = 11$)

Students' strategies evolve over time, becoming more sophisticated as the year progresses. Early in the year, second graders use familiar numbers and combinations, such as $5 + 5 = 10$. As they become accustomed to the routine, they begin to see patterns in the combinations and have favorite kinds of number sentences. Later in the year, they draw on their experiences and increased understanding of number. For example, on the forty-ninth day they might include $100 - 51$, or even $1000 - 951$ in their list of ways to make 49. The types of number sentences that students contribute over time can provide you with a window into their thinking and their levels of understanding of numbers.

If you are doing the full-year grade 2 curriculum, Today's Number is introduced in the first unit, *Mathematical Thinking at Grade 2*. Throughout the curriculum, variations are often introduced as whole-class activities and then carried on in the Start-Up section. The Start-Up section at the beginning of each session offers suggestions of variations and extensions of Today's Number.

While it is important to do Today's Number every day, it is not necessary to do it during math time. In fact, many teachers have successfully included Today's Number as part of their regular routines at the beginning or end of each day. Other teachers incorporate Today's Number into the odd 10 or 15 minutes that exist before lunch or before a transition time.

If you are teaching an *Investigations* unit for the first time, rather than using the number of days you have been in school as Today's Number, you might choose to use the calendar date. (If today is the sixteenth of the month, 16 is Today's Number.) Or you might choose to begin a counting line that does not correspond to the school day number. Each day, add a number to the strip and use this as Today's Number. Begin with the basic activity and then add variations once students become familiar with this routine.

The basic activity is described below, followed by suggested variations.

Materials

■ Chart paper
■ Student Sheet 1, Weekly Log
■ Interlocking cubes

If you are doing the basic activity, you will also need the following materials:

■ Index cards (cut in half and numbered with the days of school so far, e.g., 1 through 5 for the first week of school)
■ Strips of adding-machine tape
■ Blank 200 chart (tape two blank 100 charts together to form a 10-by-20 grid)

Continued on next page

Basic Activity

Initially, you will want to use Today's Number in a whole group, starting the first week of school. After a short time, students will be familiar with the routine and be ready to use it independently.

Establishing the Routine

Step 1. Post the chart paper.   Call students' attention to the small box on their Weekly Logs in which they have been recording the number of the days they have been in school.

Step 2. Record Today's Number.   Write the number of the day at the top of the chart paper. Ask students to suggest ways of making that total.

Step 3. List the number sentences students suggest.   Record their suggestions on chart paper. As you do so, invite the group to confirm each suggestion or discuss any incorrect responses, and to explain their thinking. You might have interlocking cubes available for students to double-check number sentences.

Step 4. Introduce the class counting strip. Show students the number cards you made and explain that the class is going to create a counting strip. Each day, the number of the day will be added to the row of cards. Post the cards in order in a visible area.

Step 5. Introduce the 200 chart.   Display the blank chart and explain that another way the class will keep track of the days in school is by filling in the chart. Record the appropriate numbers in the chart. Tell the class that each day the number of the day will be added to the chart. To help bring attention to landmark numbers on the chart, ask questions such as, "How many more days until the tenth day of school? the twentieth day?"

Variations

When students are familiar with the structure of Today's Number, you can connect it to the number work they are doing in particular units.

Make Today's Number   Ask students to use some of the following to represent the number:

- only addition
- only subtraction
- both addition and subtraction
- three numbers
- combinations of 10 ($23 = 4 + 6 + 4 + 6 + 3$ or $23 = 1 + 9 + 2 + 8 + 3$)
- a double ($36 = 18 + 18$ or $36 = 4 + 4 + 5 + 5 + 9 + 9$)
- multiples of 5 and 10 ($52 = 10 + 10 + 10 + 10 + 10 + 2$ or $52 = 5 + 15 + 20 + 10 + 2$)

Use the idea of working backward. Put the number sentences for Today's Number on the board and ask students to determine what number you are expressing: $10 + 3 + 5 + 7 + 5 + 4 = ?$ Notice how students add this string of numbers. Do they use combinations of 10 or doubles to help them?

In addition to defining how Today's Number is expressed, you can vary how and when the activity is done:

Start the Day with Today's Number   Post the day's chart paper ahead of time. When students begin arriving, they can generate number sentences and check them with partners, then record their ways to make the number of the day before school begins. Students can review the list of ways to make the number at that time or at the beginning of math class. At whole-group meeting or morning meeting, add the day's number to the 200 chart and the counting strip.

Continued on next page

Choice Time   Post chart paper with the Number of the Day written on it so that it is accessible to students. As one of their choices, students generate number sentences and check them with partners, then record them on the chart paper.

Work with a Partner   Each student works with a partner for 5 to 10 minutes and lists some ways to make the day's number. Partners check each other's work. Pairs bring their lists to the class meeting or sharing time. Students have their lists of number sentences in their math folders. These can be used as a record of students' growth in working with number over the school year.

Homework   Assign Today's Number as homework. Students share number sentences sometime during class the following day.

Catch Up   It can be easy to get a few days behind in this routine, so here are two ways to catch up. Post two or three Number-of-the-Day pages for students to visit during Choice Time or free time. Or assign a Number of the Day to individual students. Each can generate number sentences for his or her number as well as collect number sentences from classmates.

Class History   Post "special messages" below the day's number card to create a timeline about your class. Special messages can include birthdays, teeth lost, field trips, memorable events, as well as math riddles.

Today's Number Book   Collect the Today's Number charts in a *Number of the Day Book*. Arrange the pages in order, creating chapters based on 10's. Chapter 1, for example, is ways to make the numbers 1 through 10, and combinations for numbers 11–20 becomes Chapter 2.

How Many Pockets?

How Many Pockets? is one of three classroom routines presented in the grade 2 *Investigations* curriculum. Routines provide students with regular practice in important mathematical ideas such as number combinations, counting and estimating data, and concepts of time. In How Many Pockets? students collect, represent, and interpret numerical data about the number of pockets everyone in the class is wearing on a particular day. This routine often becomes known as Pocket Day. In addition to providing opportunities for comparison of data, Pocket Days provide a meaningful context in which students work purposefully with counting and grouping. Pocket Day experiences contribute to the development of students' number sense—the ability to use numbers flexibly and to see relationships among numbers.

If you are doing the full-year grade 2 curriculum, collect pocket data at regular intervals throughout the year. Many teachers collect pocket data every tenth day of school.

The basic activity is described below, followed by suggested variations. Variations are introduced within the context of the *Investigations* units. If you are not doing the full grade 2 curriculum, begin with the basic activity and then add variations when students become familiar with this routine.

Materials

- Interlocking cubes
- Large jar
- Large rubber band or tape
- Hundred Number Wall Chart and number cards (1–100)
- Pocket Data Chart (teacher made)
- Class list of names
- Chart paper

1	2	3	4	5	6	7	8	9	10
11	12	13	14	15	16	17	18	19	20
21	22	23	24	25	26	27	28	29	30
31	32	33	34	35	36	37	38	39	40
41	42	43	44	45	46	47	48	49	50
51	52	53	54	55	56	57	58	59	60
61	62	63	64	65	66	67	68	69	70
71	72	73	74	75	76	77	78	79	80
81	82	83	84	85	86	87	88	89	90
91	92	93	94	95	96	97	98	99	100

Hundred Number Wall Chart

How many pockets are we wearing today?	Pockets	People
Pocket Day 1		

Pocket Data Chart

Basic Activity

Step 1. Students estimate how many pockets the class is wearing today. Students share their estimates and their reasoning. Record the estimates on chart paper. As the Pocket Days continue through the year, students' estimates may be based on the data recorded on past Pocket Days.

Continued on next page

Step 2. Students count their pockets. Each student takes 1 interlocking cube for each pocket he or she is wearing.

Step 3. Students put the cubes representing their pockets in a large jar. Vary the way you do this. For example, rather than passing the jar around the group, call on students with specific numbers of pockets to put their cubes in the jar (e.g., students with 3 pockets). Use numeric criteria to determine who puts cubes in the jar (e.g., students with more than 5 but fewer than 8 pockets). Mark the level of cubes on the jar with a rubber band or tape.

Step 4. With students, agree on a way to count the cubes. Count the cubes to find the total number of pockets. Ask students for ideas about how to double-check the count. By recounting in another way, students see that a group of objects can be counted in more than one way; for example, by 1's, 2's, 5's, and 10's. With many experiences, they begin to realize that some ways of counting are more efficient than others, and that a group of items can be counted in ways other than by 1 without changing the total.

Primary students are usually most secure counting by 1's, and that is often their method of choice. Experiences with counting and grouping in other ways help them begin to see that number is conserved or remains the same regardless of its arrangement—20 cubes is 20 whether counted by 1's, 2's, or 5's. Students also become more flexible in their ability to use grouping, especially important in our number system, in which grouping by 10 is key.

Step 5. Record the total for the day on a Pocket Data Chart. Maintaining a chart of the pocket data as they are accumulated provides natural opportunities for students to see that data can change over time and to compare quantities.

How many pockets are we wearing today?	Pockets	People
Pocket Day 1	41	29

Variations

Comparing Data Students revisit the data from the previous Pocket Day and the corresponding cube level marked on the now empty jar.

On the last Pocket Day, we counted [*give number*] pockets. Do you think we will be wearing more, fewer, or about the same number of pockets today? Why?

After students explain their reasoning, continue with the basic activity. When the cubes have been collected, invite students to compare the present level of cubes now with the previous level indicated by the tape or rubber band and to revise their estimates based on this visual information.

Discuss the revised estimates and then complete the activity. After you add the day's total to the Pocket Data Chart, ask students to compare and interpret the data. To facilitate discussion, build a train of interlocking cubes for today's and the previous Pocket Day's number. As students compare the trains, elicit what the cube trains represent and why they have different numbers of cubes.

Use the Hundred Number Wall Chart Do the basic activity, but this time let students choose only one way to count the cubes. Then introduce the Hundred Number Wall Chart as a tool that can be used for counting cubes. This is easiest when done with students sitting on the floor in a circle.

Continued on next page

To check our pocket count, we'll put our cubes in the pockets on the chart. A pocket can have just one cube, so we'll put one cube in number 1's pocket, the next cube in number 2's pocket, and keep going in the same way. How many cubes can we put in the first row?

Students will probably see that 10 cubes will fill the first row of the chart.

One group of 10 cubes fits in this row. What if we complete the second row? How many rows of the chart do you think we will fill with the cubes we counted today?

Encourage students to share their thinking. Then have them count with you and help to place the cubes one by one in the pockets on the chart. When finished, examine the chart together, pointing out the total number of cubes in it and the number of complete rows. For each row, snap together the cubes to make a train of 10. As you do so, use the rows to encourage students to consider combining groups of 10. Record the day's total on your Pocket Data Chart.

Note: If cubes do not fit in the pockets of the chart, place the chart on the floor and place the cubes on top of the numbers.

Find the Most Common Number of Pockets
Each student connects the cubes representing his or her pockets into a train. Before finding the total number of pockets, sort the cube trains with students to find the most common number of pockets. Pose and investigate additional questions too, such as:

- **How many people are wearing the greatest number of pockets?**

- **Is there a number of pockets no one is wearing?**

- **Who has the fewest pockets?**

The cubes are then counted to determine the total number of pockets.

Take a Closer Look at Pocket Data Each student builds a cube train representing his or her pockets. Beginning with those who have zero pockets, call on students to bring their cube trains to the front of the room. Record the information in a chart, such as the one shown here. You might make a permanent chart with blanks for placing number cards.

Pose questions about the data, such as, "Two people have 2 pockets. How many pockets is that?" Then record the number of pockets.

_0_ people have 0 pockets.	_0 pockets_
_4_ people have 1 pocket.	_4 pockets_
_2_ people have 2 pockets.	_4 pockets_
_2_ people have 3 pockets.	_6 pockets_

To work with combining groups, you might keep a running total of pockets as data are recorded in the chart until you have found the cumulative total.

We counted [12] pockets, and then we counted [6] pockets. How many pockets have we counted so far? Be ready to tell us how you thought about it.

As students give their solutions, encourage them to share their mental strategies. Alternatively, after all data have been collected, students can work on the problem of finding the total number of pockets.

Graph Pocket Data Complete the activity using the variation Find the Most Common Number of Pockets. Leave students' cube trains intact. Each student then creates a representation of the day's pocket data. Provide a variety of materials including stick-on notes, stickers or paper squares, markers and crayons, drawing paper, and graph paper for students to use.

Continued on next page

These cube trains represent how many pockets people are wearing today. Suppose you want to show our pocket data to your family, friends, or students in another classroom. How could you show our pocket data on paper so that someone else could see what we found out about our pockets today?

By creating their own representations, students become more familiar with the data and may begin to develop theories as they consider how to communicate what they know about the data to an audience. Students' representations may not be precise; what's important is that the representations enable them to describe and interpret their data.

Compare Pocket Data with Another Class

Arrange ahead of time to compare pocket data with a fourth- or fifth-grade class. Present the following question to students:

Do you think fifth-grade students wear more, fewer, or about the same number of pockets as second-grade students? Why?

Discuss students' thinking. Then investigate this question by comparing your data with data from another classroom. One way to do this is to invite the other class to participate in your Pocket Day. Do the activity first with the second graders, recording on the Pocket Data Chart how many people have each number of pockets and finding the total number of pockets. Repeat with the other students, recording their data on chart paper. Then compare the two sets of data.

How does the number of pockets in the fifth grade compare to the number of pockets in second grade?

Discuss students' ideas.

Calculate the Total Number of Pockets Divide students into groups of four or five. Each group determines the total number of pockets being worn by the group. Data from each small group are shared and recorded on the board. Using this information, students work in pairs to determine the total number of pockets worn by the class. As a group, they share strategies used for determining the total number of pockets.

In another variation, students share individual pocket data with the group. Each student records this information using a class list of names to keep track. They then determine the total number of pockets worn by the students in the class. Observe how students calculate the total number of pockets. What materials do they use? Do they group familiar numbers together, such as combinations of 10, doubles, or multiples of 5?

Time and Time Again

Time and Time Again is one of three classroom routines included in the grade 2 *Investigations* curriculum. This routine helps students develop an understanding of time-related ideas such as sequencing of events, the passage of time, duration of time periods, and identifying important times in their day.

Because many of the ideas and suggestions presented in this routine will be incorporated throughout the school day and into other parts of the curriculum, we encourage teachers to use this routine in whatever way meets the needs of their students and their classroom. We believe that learning about time and understanding ideas about time happen best when activities are presented *over* time and have relevance to students' experiences and lives.

Daily Schedule   Post a daily schedule. Identify important times (start of school, math, music, recess, reading) using both analog (clockface) and digital (10:15) representations. Discuss the daily schedule each day and encourage students to compare the actual starting time of, say, math class with what is posted on the schedule.

Talk Time   Identify times as you talk with students. For example, "In 15 minutes we will be cleaning up and going to recess." Include specific times and refer to a clock in your classroom: "It is now 10:15. In 15 minutes we will be cleaning up and going out to recess. That will be at 10:30."

Timing One Hour   Set a timer to go off at 1-hour intervals. Choose a starting time and write both the analog time (use a clockface) and the digital time. When the timer rings, record the time using analog and digital times. At the end of the day, students make observations about the data collected. Initially you'll want to use whole and half hours as your starting points. Gradually you can use times that are 10 or 20 minutes after the hour and also appoint students to be in charge of the timer and of recording the times.

Timing Other Intervals   Set a timer to go off at 15-minute intervals over a period of 2 hours. Begin at the hour and after the data have been collected, discuss with students what happened each time 15 minutes was added to the time (11:00, 11:15, 11:30, 11:45). You can also try this with 10-minute intervals.

Home Schedule   Students make a schedule of important times at home. They can do this both for school days and for nonschool days. They should include both analog and digital times on their schedules. Later in the year they can use this schedule to see if they were really on time for things like dinner, piano lessons, or bedtime. They record the actual time that events happened and calculate how early or late they were. Students can illustrate their schedules.

Comparing Schedules   Partners compare important times in their day, such as what time they eat dinner, go to bed, get up, leave for school. They can compare whether events are earlier or later, and some students might want to calculate how much earlier or later these events occur.

Life Timeline   Students create a timeline of their lives. They interview family members and collect information about important developmental milestones such as learning to walk, first word, first day of school, first lost tooth, and important family events. Students then record these events on a timeline that is a representation of the first seven or eight years of their lives.

Clock Data   Students collect data about the types of clocks they have in their home—digital or analog. They make a representation of these data and as a class compare their results.

- Are there more digital or analog clocks in your house?
- Is this true of our class set of data?
- How could we compare our individual data to a class set of data?

Continued on next page

Time Collection   Students bring in things from home that have to do with time. Include digital and analog clocks as well as timers of various sorts. These items could be sorted and grouped in different ways. Some students may be interested in investigating different types of timepieces such as sundials, sand timers, and pendulums.

How Long Is a Minute?   As you time 1 minute, students close their eyes and then raise their hands when they think a minute has gone by. Ask, "Is a minute longer or shorter than you imagined?" Repeat this activity or have students do this with partners. You can also do this activity with a half-minute.

What Can You Do in a Minute?   When students are familiar with timing 1 minute, they work in pairs and collect data about things they can do in 1 minute. Brainstorm a list of events that students might try. Some ideas that second graders have suggested include: writing their names; doing jumping jacks or sit-ups; hopping on one foot; saying the ABC's; snapping together interlocking cubes; writing certain numbers or letters (this is great practice for working on reversals); and drawing geometric shapes such as triangles, squares, or stars. Each student chooses four or five activities to do in 1 minute. Before they collect the data, they predict how many they can do in 1 minute. Then with partners they gather the data and compare.

How Long Does It Take?   Using a stopwatch or a clock with a second hand, time how long it takes students to complete certain tasks such as lining up, giving out supplies, or cleaning up after math time. Emphasize doing these things in a responsible way. Students can take turns being "timekeepers."

Stopwatches   Most second graders are fascinated by stopwatches. You will find that students come up with many ideas about what to time. If possible, acquire a stopwatch for your classroom. (Inexpensive ones are available through educational supply catalogs.) Having stopwatches available in the classroom allows students to teach each other about time and how to keep track of time.

The following activities will help ensure that this unit is comprehensible to students who are acquiring English as a second language. The suggested approach is based on *The Natural Approach: Language Acquisition in the Classroom* by Stephen D. Krashen and Tracy D. Terrell (Alemany Press, 1983.) The intent is for second-language learners to acquire new vocabulary in an active, meaningful context.

Note that *acquiring* a word is different from *learning* a word. Depending on their level of proficiency, students may be able to comprehend a word upon hearing it during an investigation, without being able to say it. Other students may be able to use the word orally, but not read or write it. The goal is to help students naturally acquire targeted vocabulary at their present level of proficiency.

We suggest using these activities just before the related investigations. The activities can be led by English-proficient students.

Investigation 1

story, beginning, what happened next

1. Read aloud a short book that has a lot of pictures and a minimal amount of words. Read the story through once. Go through the book a second time. Ask students straightforward questions as they look at each picture, "Who is this?" "What does the wolf want to do?" "Whom did the wolf meet?"

2. Ask students questions about the beginning and end of the story. "At the beginning of the story [*point to the first few pages*] was the wolf inside or outside the pig's house? At the end of the story [*point to the last few pages*], were the pigs happy or sad?

3. Ask students questions about the sequence of events in the story. "After the wolf left the first pig's house, what happened next? Did he go the the store? Did he go to another pig's house?" Remember, questions should be simple and require only one- or two-word responses.

Investigation 2

how far away, finish a row

1. Arrange 5 or 6 chairs in a row in front of the class and ask students to come up and sit in them. Ask questions about how far away students are from one another. "How far is Juan from Rose? Is he 2 chairs away? Is he 4 chairs away?"

2. Line up different-colored buttons (or other small objects) on a table. Ask students questions about how far one button is from another one. "How far away is the green button from the red button? Is it 1 button away? Is it 3 buttons away?"

3. Place about seven buttons in a row on a blank 100 chart. Then point to the three remaining spaces of the row. Tell students that you need three more buttons to finish the row. Then place the remaining buttons and show students the completed row.

4. Start placing buttons on another row. Ask students to decide how many more buttons are needed to finish that row. Count the empty spaces together, then fill in the rest of the row with buttons.

5. Ask student volunteers to take turns placing a number of buttons on a row and calling on others to tell how many more are needed to finish the row.

Blackline Masters

Investigation 5

General Resources for the Unit

_____ , 19 ____

Dear Family,

During the next few weeks in math class, we will be working on addition and subtraction. We will be working with 5's, 10's, 20's, and 25's and on ways to make 100. We will also work on solving story problems and deciding what operation to use to solve a problem.

While our class is working on this unit, you can help in several ways:

- Encourage your child to use his or her own strategies for addition and subtraction. We will use many strategies in class.

- For homework, your child will be writing various types of story problems. Ask your child to tell you about strategies he or she uses to solve these problems. Encourage your child to use words, pictures, and numbers in any explanation.

- Your child will also be bringing home some of the games that we are playing during math class. Take some time to play these games with your child.

- Children will be working with problems involving money. Use some change to investigate ways to make $1 or $2 with your child.

- Look for addition and subtraction situations at home and share them with your child. For example, if you bake a batch of cookies and you set some aside for school lunches, how many cookies will be left for the family to eat? You and your child might compare the ages of the people in your family: How much older are you than your child? Or if you have 26¢ in your pocket and you want to buy a snack that costs 55¢, how much more money do you need?

The one thing to keep in mind with these problems is the size of the numbers. Numbers under 100 are about the right size for most second graders. Some children may be comfortable using counters (beans, buttons or pennies) to solve problems, while others might want to write their thinking on paper or solve problems mentally.

We will be encouraging all of these approaches as the children work with addition and subtraction in class.

Thank you for your help.

Sincerely,

Weekly Log

Day Box

Monday, _____	
Tuesday, _____	
Wednesday, _____	
Thursday, _____	
Friday, _____	

Story Problems, Set A

Solve these problems. Explain your strategies using pictures, numbers, or words.

1. A class of 29 students is going on a trip to the science museum. There are 12 adults going with them. How many people are going on the trip?

2. Next week other students will go to the science museum. There will be 39 students and 12 adults. How many people will go on this trip?

An Addition Story Problem

Write and solve a story problem about an addition situation. Your story problem can be about anything that you might see out your window at home. Show your thinking using words, numbers, and pictures. You may use the back of this sheet if necessary.

Story Problems, Set B

Solve these problems. Explain your strategies using pictures, numbers, or words.

1. Yesterday at the park, I counted 39 pigeons. When a big dog walked by, 17 of them flew away. How many were still there?

2. Today I went to the park again. I counted 39 pigeons. A big dog barked and 16 of them flew away. How many were still there?

A Subtraction Story Problem

Write and solve a story problem about a subtraction situation. Your story problem can be about anything that you might see out your window at home. Show your thinking using words, numbers, and pictures. You may use the back of this sheet if necessary.

Story Problems, Set D

Solve these problems. Explain your strategies using pictures, numbers, or words.

1. Jake collects stamps. He had 32 stamps. His sister gave him some more. Now he has 48. How many did his sister give him?

_____

2. Kira had 40 marbles. She gave some to her best friend. Now she has 28 marbles left. How many did she give to her friend?

Discussing Addition and Subtraction

Ask an adult in your household when he or she uses
addition or subtraction. It might help to think about
cooking, driving, shopping, or paying bills.

_____

_____

_____

_____

_____

_____

_____

_____

_____

_____

_____

Problem Strategies

Here's the problem I am solving:

Here's how I solved it:

Here's the problem I am solving:

Here's how I solved it:

Writing and Solving a Story Problem

Write and solve a story problem about either an addition or subtraction situation. Your story problem can be about anything that interests you. Show your thinking using words, numbers, and pictures. You may use the back of this sheet if necessary.

1. On Saturday, Kira and Jake counted animals in the park. They counted 23 pigeons and 37 squirrels. How many animals did they count?

2. Kira and Jake went for a walk. They counted 25 pigeons and 35 squirrels. How many animals did they count?

3. Kira and Jake fed bread crumbs to the birds in the pond. There were 16 ducks and 26 geese. How many birds were there?

4. One day, there were 26 ducks and 36 geese at the pond. How many birds were there?

5. On Monday there was a bicycle race in the park. There were 25 children and 18 adults in the race. How many people were in the race?

6. On Sunday, there was a kite-flying contest. There were 28 children and 15 adults flying kites. How many people were flying kites?

7. Kira planted 41 flowers in the fall. In the spring, 27 of them came up. How many flowers did not come up?

8. Kira's mother has 41 tomatoes that grew in her garden. She gave 17 of them to neighbors. Kira's family ate the rest. How many tomatoes did Kira's family eat?

9. In Jake's garden, 33 flowers came up. There are 15 tulips. The rest are daffodils. How many are daffodils?

10. In Kira's garden, 43 flowers came up. There are 25 tulips. The rest are daffodils. How many are daffodils?

11. In Kira's garden there were 45 daisies. Rabbits ate 29 of them. How many daisies are left?

12. Kira had 46 daisies in her garden. She picked 30 to give to her father. How many were left?

1. Jake baked 24 cookies. Jake's mom baked some more. Then they had 48 cookies. How many did Jake's mom bake?

2. Jake and his mom baked 48 cookies. Jake ate 5 cookies, his sister ate 5 cookies, and his mom ate some. There are 35 cookies left. How many cookies did Jake's mom eat?

3. Kira earned 25¢ doing errands for her grandfather. She earned some more doing errands for her aunt. She earned 40¢ altogether. How much money did Kira's aunt pay her?

4. Jake earned 35¢ for cleaning the yard. His grandmother paid him to walk the dog. Now Jake has 50¢. How much did his grandmother pay him?

Investigation 1 • Resource
Putting Together and Taking Apart

Student Sheet 10

1	2	3	4	5	6	7	8	9	10
11	12	13	14	15	16	17	18	19	20
21	22	23	24	25	26	27	28	29	30
31	32	33	34	35	36	37	38	39	40
41	42	43	44	45	46	47	48	49	50
51	52	53	54	55	56	57	58	59	60
61	62	63	64	65	66	67	68	69	70
71	72	73	74	75	76	77	78	79	80
81	82	83	84	85	86	87	88	89	90
91	92	93	94	95	96	97	98	99	100

Side-by-Side 100 Charts

1	2	3	4	5	6	7	8	9	10
11	12	13	14	15	16	17	18	19	20
21	22	23	24	25	26	27	28	29	30
31	32	33	34	35	36	37	38	39	40
41	42	43	44	45	46	47	48	49	50
51	52	53	54	55	56	57	58	59	60
61	62	63	64	65	66	67	68	69	70
71	72	73	74	75	76	77	78	79	80
81	82	83	84	85	86	87	88	89	90
91	92	93	94	95	96	97	98	99	100

Multiples-of-5 Cards

5	5	5	5
10	10	10	10
15	15	15	15
20	20	30	30
5	5	10	10

Get to 100

Materials: Multiples-of-5 number cubes (2) or set of Multiples-of-5 Cards, 100 chart (for each player), game piece (for each player), paper

Players: 2 to 3

How to Play

The object of the game is to reach 100 on the 100 chart.

1. Each player puts a game piece to the left of number 1.

2. Take turns. Roll the number cubes or draw two number cards and move that many spaces on the 100 chart.

3. Record your move on paper. For example, if your first roll is 5 and 15, write 5 + 15.

   If your next roll is 10 + 5, move that many spaces and add these numbers to your recording so that you have 5 + 15 + 10 + 5. Your game piece should be at 35.

4. Continue play, recording your moves each time.

5. You can use just one of the amounts on the number cubes or cards to land directly on 100.

6. When you reach 100, check your moves by adding all the numbers on your paper. If the sum does not equal 100, move your game piece back to the total number and continue play.

7. If the numbers do add to 100, move your game piece back and play again.

Pinching Paper Clips

1. I pinched _____ paper clips.
   There are _____ paper clips left in the box.
   Here's how I figured this out.

_____

2. I pinched _____ paper clips.
   There are _____ paper clips left in the box.
   Here's how I figured this out.

_____

3. I pinched _____ paper clips.
   There are _____ paper clips left in the box.
   Here's how I figured this out.

Pinching Objects

Fill a bag or bowl with 100 small objects such as beans, pennies, or buttons.

1. I pinched _____ _____ . There are _____ _____ left.
             (number) (object name)   (number) (object name)
    Here's how I figured this out.

---

2. I pinched _____ _____ . There are _____ _____ left.
             (number) (object name)   (number) (object name)
    Here's how I figured this out.

Optional: Take two or three pinches. Figure out how many are left.

How Many Paper Clips?

Solve this problem. Explain your strategy using pictures, numbers, or words.

Franco has 63 paper clips and he needs to fill the box with 100 paper clips. How many more paper clips does he need to add to the box?

Check your solution by solving the problem in a different way. Explain the strategy you used to check.

Writing and Solving Story Problems About 100

Use your collection of 100 small objects to write and solve a story problem about 100. Show your thinking using words, numbers, and pictures. You may use the back of this sheet if necessary.

How many cubes do you have in all?

How many more cubes do you need to finish another row of 10?

How far from 50 cubes are you?

How many cubes do you have? TAKE 10 cubes.

Now how many cubes do you have?

How many cubes do you need to add or take away so that you have 50 cubes in all?

Roll the number cubes again. TAKE double the number of cubes.

How many cubes do you have in all?	How many more cubes do you need to finish another row of 10?
How many cubes do you have? GIVE BACK 10 cubes. Now how many cubes do you have?	How many cubes do you have? TAKE 5 extra cubes. How many cubes do you have now?
Roll the number cubes again. TAKE double the number of cubes.	How many cubes do you have? TAKE another 10 cubes. How many cubes do you have now?

1. Jake has 73 pennies. When he gets 100 pennies he can trade them for $1. How many more pennies does Jake need?

2. Kira had 100 pennies. She spent 119 pennies on an apple. How many pennies does Kira have left?

3. Kira and Jake were playing Get to 100. Kira's marker was on 65. How far is Kira from 100?

4. In the game Get to 100, Jake's marker was on 35. How much more does Jake need to get to 100?

Investigation 2 • Resource
Putting Together and Taking Apart

5. Harris has a collection of 100 marbles. He gave some to his brother. Now he has 71 marbles left. How many did Harris give to his brother?

6. A bowl had 100 jelly beans. Jeffrey took a handful from the bowl. Now there are 82 jelly beans left in the bowl. How many did Jeffrey take?

7. Ebony and Simon want to make 100 paper hearts. Ebony has made 47 hearts and Simon has made 43 hearts. Have they made enough hearts?

If not, how many more should they make?

8. Laura had 27¢ in her pocket. Then she earned 25¢ for walking the dog and 45¢ for washing the dishes. How much money does Laura have now?

How much more money does Laura need to earn to have $1?

Cover-Up Recording Sheet

Total Number	Number Not Covered	Number Covered
_____	_____	_____
_____	_____	_____
_____	_____	_____
_____	_____	_____
_____	_____	_____
_____	_____	_____
_____	_____	_____
_____	_____	_____
_____	_____	_____

Story Problems, Set F

Solve these problems. Explain your strategies using pictures, numbers, or words.

1. Mrs. Lee had 46 goldfish in her pet store. She sold some of the goldfish. Now she has 25 left. How many goldfish did Mrs. Lee sell?

---

2. Mrs. Lee had 46 mice in her pet store. She sold some of the mice. Now she has 27 mice left. How many mice did she sell?

1. Jake and Kira were playing Cover-Up. They had 45 buttons. Jake covered some up. Kira could still see 28. How many buttons did Jake cover?

2. Kira had a pile of 28 buttons. Jake put some more buttons in the pile. Then they had 43 buttons. How many buttons did Jake put in the pile?

3. Kira and Jake have 50¢. If they share a soda that costs 29¢, how much money will they have left?

4. Kira bought a soda for 29¢ and Jake bought a juice for 25¢. How much money did they spend?

5. Jake had 25¢. He found 11¢ in his room. He earned 40¢ more for shoveling snow. How much does he have now?

6. Kira had 76¢. She bought some apples and got 25¢ change. How much did the apples cost?

7. Kira collects shells. She found 25 of them on the beach. Her grandfather gave her some more. Now she has 41 shells. How many shells did her grandfather give her?

8. Jake had 35¢ in his pocket. He dropped 17¢ when it fell through a hole in his pocket. How much money does Jake have now?

9. Kira wants to buy a book that costs $1. She has 72¢. How much more does she need?

10. Jake took $1 to the store. He bought an eraser for 39¢ and a pencil for 35¢. How much change did he get?

$35 + 27 =$ _____

$63 - 18 =$ _____

$41 +$ _____ $= 66$

$52 -$ _____ $= 31$

$25 + 57 =$ _____

$41 - 13 =$ _____

$16 +$ _____ $= 72$

$56 -$ _____ $= 38$

_____ $+ 13 = 70$

$100 -$ _____ $= 85$

Ways to Make 100

Make 100 in as many ways as you can. Think
of at least five ways. You might want to use your
collection of 100 small objects. Make sure to show your
solutions and how you reached them!

Ways to Make $1

Make $1 in as many ways as you can using nickels, dimes, and quarters. Record your answer using numbers, pictures, and/or words.

Comparing Story Problems

Show how you solved the problem. Use words, pictures, or numbers.

1. Kira and Jake are playing marbles. Kira has 40 marbles and Jake has 26. How many more marbles does Kira have than Jake?

_____

2. Jake played marbles with some friends. He started with 26 marbles. At the end of the game he had 48 marbles. How many marbles did Jake win?

A Comparing Story Problem

Think about a situation where you might compare two amounts. Write and solve a story problem that compares two numbers. Show your thinking using words, numbers, and pictures.

Capture 5 Recording Sheet

Record your starting number, the changes you use, and your ending number for each move, like this:

$$16 + 10 + 10 - 2 = 34$$

_____

_____

_____

_____

_____

_____

_____

_____

_____

_____

Change Cards (1-3)

+1	+1	+1	+1
−1	−1	−1	−1
+2	+2	+2	+2
−2	−2	−2	−2
+3	+3	−3	−3

Change Cards (10–30)

+10	+10	+10	+10
−10	−10	−10	−10
+20	+20	+20	+20
−20	−20	−20	−20
+30	+30	−30	−30

Capture 5

Materials: 100 chart, deck of Change Cards, 12 markers of one color, game piece for each player, paper

Players: Two players or two teams

How to Play

The object of the game is to collect 5 game markers.

1. Place 12 markers on the 100 chart, so each marker is on a different number. Deal 5 Change Cards to each player or team and place the remaining cards face down. Players put their game pieces anywhere on the 100 chart.

2. On a turn, move your game piece using any combination of your Change Cards to land on a square with a marker. You can use any number of cards from 1 to 5.

3. If you land exactly on a square with a marker, capture it by taking it off the board. You can only capture one marker during a turn, and it must be the last square you land on.

4. Record your moves in an equation. If you begin on 45, and use the cards: +2, +10, +3, you record: $45 + 2 + 10 + 3 = 60$.

5. Place the Change Cards you used face down in a discard pile. Take cards from the top of the deck to replace them. If the deck of Change Cards is used up, shuffle the discard pile and turn it face down again.

6. The first player or team to capture 5 markers wins.

Capture 5 Equations

1. Linda's marker was on 21 and she captured a marker on 47. She wrote this equation: $21 + 2 + 3 + 1 + 20 = 47$. How many spaces did Linda move? Explain how you figured this out.

   Rewrite Linda's equation to show how far she moved:

   $21 + \underline{\quad} = 47$

2. Ping's marker was on 58 and he captured a marker on 92. He wrote this equation: $58 + 2 + 30 + 2 = 92$. How many spaces did Ping move? Explain how you figured this out.

   Rewrite Ping's equation to show how far he moved: _____

3. Jeffrey's marker was on 9 and he captured a marker on 37. He wrote this equation: $9 + 20 + 3 + 2 + 3 = 37$. How many spaces did Jeffrey move? Explain how you figured this out.

   Rewrite Jeffrey's equation to show how far he moved: _____

Alphabet Addition

Make five words and use the code in the chart below to figure out how much each word is worth. Show how you figured out how much each word is worth.

All consonants are worth 5, except for J, Q, V, W, X, and Z.

All vowels are worth 10.

J, Q, V, W, X, and Z are worth 15.

A = 10	G = 5	M = 5	S = 5	Y = 5
B = 5	H = 5	N = 5	T = 5	Z = 15
C = 5	I = 10	O = 10	U = 10	
D = 5	J = 15	P = 5	V = 15	
E = 10	K = 5	Q = 15	W = 15	
F = 5	L = 5	R = 5	X – 15	

How Far?

1. How far is it from 38 to 65? How do you know?
   Explain your thinking using words and numbers.

_____

2. How far is it from 52 to 29? How do you know?
   Explain your thinking using words and numbers.

1. Kira has 36 marbles and Jake has 58 marbles. How many more marbles does Kira have than Jake?

2. Kira and Jake went to the post office to buy three stamps. Each stamp cost 32¢. How much money did they need?

3. Kira and Jake want to buy three apples. Each apple costs 33¢. Kira has 44¢ and Jake has 35¢. Do they have enough money to buy three apples?

   Will they have any money left or will they need more? How much?

4. Jake is making a birthday cake for his mom. She will be 42 years old. Jake only has 27 candles. How many more candles does he need?

5. The pet store had a large tank filled with 100 goldfish. Kira bought 23 and Jake bought 19. How many goldfish were left at the pet store?

6. Jake and his dad blew up 60 balloons for his mom's party. Jake's cat Roo popped 23 balloons with his claws. How many balloons were left?

7. Jake and Kira each collected cans for recycling. Jake collected 48 cans in all. He collected 12 more than Kira. How many cans did Kira collect?

8. Two classes of students went to the park. There was a total of 64 students. One class had 33 students. How many students were in the other class?

1. Kira had 48¢ in her pocket. Her big brother gave her 25¢ for running an errand. Now how much does she have?

2. Jake has 23¢ in his pocket. Kira has 25¢ more than Jake. How much money does Kira have?

3. Kira and Jake were riding the bus. They counted 33 people on the bus. More people got on. Now there are 62 people on the bus. How many more people got on the bus?

4. There are 53 people on the bus. There are 27 adults. The rest are children. How many are children?

5. Kira wants to buy a pen. She sees a red one that costs 48¢. She also sees one with sparkles for 65¢. How much more does the one with sparkles cost?

6. Kira chooses a pen with stars. She pays for it with three quarters. She gets 10¢ change. How much does the pen cost?

1	2	3	4	5	6	7	8	9	10
11	12	13	14	15	16	17	18	19	20
21	22	23	24	25	26	27	28	29	30
31	32	33	34	35	36	37	38	39	40
41	42	43	44	45	46	47	48	49	50
51	52	53	54	55	56	57	58	59	60
61	62	63	64	65	66	67	68	69	70
71	72	73	74	75	76	77	78	79	80
81	82	83	84	85	86	87	88	89	90
91	92	93	94	95	96	97	98	99	100

Practice Pages

This optional section provides homework ideas for teachers who want or need to give more homework than is assigned to accompany the activities in this unit. The problems included here provide additional practice in learning about number relationships and in solving computation and number problems. For number units, you may want to use some of these if your students need more work in these areas or if you want to assign daily homework. For other units, you can use these problems so that students can continue to work on developing number and computation sense while they are focusing on other mathematical content in class. We recommend that you introduce activities in class before assigning related problems for homework.

Tens Go Fish   Students play this game in the units *Mathematical Thinking at Grade 2* and *Coins, Coupons, and Combinations*. If your students are familiar with the game, you can simply send home the directions and Number Cards so that students can play at home. If your students have not played the game before, introduce it in class and have students play once or twice before sending it home. You might have students do this activity four times for homework in this unit.

Close to 20   Students are introduced to this game in *Coins, Coupons, and Combinations*. If your students are familiar with the game, you can simply send home the directions, score sheet, and Number Cards so that students can play at home. If your students have not played the game before, introduce it in class and have students play once or twice before sending it home. You might have students do this activity four times for homework in this unit.

Story Problems   Story problems at various levels of difficulty are used throughout the *Investigations* curriculum. The two story problem sheets provided here help students review and maintain skills that have already been taught. You can make up other problems in this format, using numbers and contexts that are appropriate for your students. Students solve the problems and then record their strategies, using numbers, words, and pictures.

People and Pet Riddles   This type of problem is introduced in the unit *Coins, Coupons, and Combinations*. Here, two problem sheets are provided. You can also make up other problems in this format, using numbers that are appropriate for your students. For each problem sheet, students solve the problem and then record their strategies, using numbers, words, or pictures.

Tens Go Fish

Materials: Deck of Number Cards 0–10 (four of each) with the wild cards removed

Players: 3 to 4

How to Play

The object of the game is to get two cards that total 10.

1. Each player is dealt five cards. The rest of the cards are placed face down in the center of the table.

2. If you have any pairs of cards that total 10, put them down in front of you and replace those cards with cards from the deck.

3. Take turns. On a turn, ask <u>one</u> other player for a card that will go with a card in your hand to make 10.

4. If you get a card that makes 10, put the pair of cards down. Take one card from the deck. Your turn is over.

   If you do not get a card that makes 10, take the top card from the deck. Your turn is over.

   If the card you take from the deck makes 10 with a card in your hand, put the pair down and take another card.

5. If there are no cards left in your hand but still cards in the deck, you take two cards.

6. The game is over when there are no more cards.

7. At the end of the game, make a list of the number pairs you made.

Close to 20

Materials: Deck of Number Cards 0–10 (four of each) with the wild cards removed; Close to 20 Score Sheet; counters

Players: 2 to 3

How to Play

The object of the game is to choose three cards that total as close to 20 as possible.

1. Deal five cards to each player.

2. Take turns. Use any three of your cards to make a total that is as close to 20 as possible.

3. Write these numbers and the total on the Close to 20 Score Sheet.

4. Find your score. The score for the round is the difference between the total and 20. For example, if you choose 8 + 7 + 3, your total is 18 and your score for the round is 2.

5. After you record your score, take that many counters.

6. Put the cards you used in a discard pile and deal three new cards to each player. If you run out of cards before the end of the game, shuffle the discard pile and use those cards again.

7. After five rounds, total your score and count your counters. These two numbers should be the same. The player with the lowest score and the fewest counters is the winner.

Close to 20 Score Sheet

PLAYER 1   SCORE

Round 1: _____ + _____ + _____ = _____   _____

Round 2: _____ + _____ + _____ = _____   _____

Round 3: _____ + _____ + _____ = _____   _____

Round 4: _____ + _____ + _____ = _____   _____

Round 5: _____ + _____ + _____ = _____   _____

TOTAL SCORE   _____

PLAYER 2   SCORE

Round 1: _____ + _____ + _____ = _____   _____

Round 2: _____ + _____ + _____ = _____   _____

Round 3: _____ + _____ + _____ = _____   _____

Round 4: _____ + _____ + _____ = _____   _____

Round 5: _____ + _____ + _____ = _____   _____

TOTAL SCORE   _____

0	0	0	0
1	1	1	1
2	2	2	2

Practice Page
Putting Together and Taking Apart

3	**3**	**3**	**3**
4	**4**	**4**	**4**
5	**5**	**5**	**5**

Practice Page
Putting Together and Taking Apart

6	6	6	6
7	7	7	7
8	8	8	8

Practice Page
Putting Together and Taking Apart

9	9	9	9
10	10	10	10
Wild Card	Wild Card	Wild Card	Wild Card

Practice Page
Putting Together and Taking Apart

Practice Page A

There are _____ students in our class.

We have 40 cups for water.

Are there enough for the class? _____

How many leftovers will we have? _____

Explain how you figured this out. You can use numbers, words, or pictures.

Practice Page B

There are _____ students in our class.

We have 31 rulers.

Are there enough for the class? _____

How many leftovers will we have? _____

Explain how you figured this out. You can use numbers, words, or pictures.

Practice Page C

There are 10 legs in this group.
There are 4 heads in this group.
There are 8 ears in this group.
There are 30 fingers in this group.
There is 1 tail in this group.

Who could be in this group?

Show how you solved this problem. You can use numbers, words, or pictures.

Practice Page D

There are 12 legs in this group.
There are 4 heads in this group.
There are 8 ears in this group.
There are 20 fingers in this group
There are 2 tails in this group.

Who could be in this group?

Show how you solved this problem. You can
use numbers, words, or pictures.